Streetwise Extreme
Surviving
the Unexpected

Streetwise Extreme Surviving the Unexpected

Frank Marchante

Grass Publishing, Miami, Florida

Streetwise Extreme Surviving the Unexpected

Published by Gras Publishing Company
www.graspublishing.com
Miami, Florida, 33155

Copyright © 2019 Frank Marchante
Cover Design by Michelle Marchante
Cover Photograph Copyright © Frank Marchante

Library of Congress Cataloging-in-Publication Data has been applied for.
Marchante, Frank
P. 285
ISBN-978-0-9779O40-8-2
613.8'5-dc22

This book is printed in Acid free paper.
United States -
Printed in the United States of America

1- Personal Self-defense 2-Safety Awareness- 3- College Campus Safety
4-Riots- 5-Terrorism- 6 - Cyber-Safety-7- Flash Roadway Mob
8- Sex Attacks- 9- Action-10- Biography

All that I am, or hope to be, I owe to my angel mother
Abraham Lincoln

Warning- Disclaimer

Dedication

I want to dedicate this book to the most important people in my life: my family. I was raised in the greatest of homes. My parents made tremendous sacrifices when they took my sister and me out of Cuba to live in freedom 57 years ago. My mother sacrificed never seeing her parents alive again for us. I am thankful to her for her strengths; she taught me morality, and encouraged me to be confident and enjoy life and taught me by example. I credit my mother for my moral, intellectual and all aspects of my life for the way she raised me.

My dad was a source of strength. I used to see him so tall and as a hero. He was my teacher, my best friend and my role model. He taught me boxing and I learned perseverance from him as well as how to be honest and hardworking. My dad will always be my superhero.

My two beautiful daughters, Monica and Michelle. When Monica was younger she knew me more than anybody and could look at my eyes and know exactly what I was thinking, we were inseparable. Michelle, who inherited her passion for writing and reading from me, and gave me very helpful comments for the book. Monica & Michelle, my daughters may have outgrown my lap, but they will never outgrow my heart.

My sister Babie, the best thing about having her as a sister is that I always have a friend, in good and bad times. We will always be tight forever.

My son, Franky. When I look at my son Franky, I see my own reflection in him, only younger. He is my life, my pride, my joy and I love my son more than anything. I am proud of him.

I would also like to dedicate this book to my wife and best friend Gilda. My grand-kids Jorgie, Sofia, Alli and Ayla.

And to all the students, especially my helpers, who used to call themselves Marchante's Mafia (like Elvis Presley's Mafia) forever in my mind and heart will be the incredible students whom I've shared my life with. All of you will always be a part of me.

Acknowledgments

Special thanks to Michelle Marchante who contributed photos for this book, the cover design and valuable tips with her expertise and experience. I'm thankful to my wife Gilda for her assistance. I would be insensible if I don't mention my companion, my dog Bella. I consulted a wide variety of sources, including books, magazine articles, and newspapers, FBI files, Government Data Base, online databases and writing articles by professional people in the field of self-defense. Any attempt to credit everyone would be impossible.

The research for this book took many months of digging thought my notes archives, reading thought reams of paper notes I have kept.

Thanks to all my students who provided me with some of the raw material that went into this book.

Many thanks.

Chapter 1..13

Introduction- Knowledge is power!!
Street Wise Extreme
Defensive Awareness
Attacks-street smart
More than one person attack
De-escalation the situation
Observable threat
Men surprise attack
Different kinds of criminal
Street Tactics
Bullies

Three responses to dangerous situation
Sucker punch
Diffuse an aggressive situation
After the confrontation
Mental condition-be ready
Recognize and Avoid Violent situations
The criminal silent weapons
The four principles of self defense
Self-defense for men

Chapter 2..59

The elevator/stairs/parking
The FBI's report: America's 15 most dangerous States.
The FBI's 10 Most Dangerous Cities in 2017
Recent FBI crimes report
The Most Dangerous Neighborhoods in America/ International
Traveling Smart
FBI's Uniform Crime Reporting
How I kept safe in these cities
Pickpockets
Tips for Women/ Men Travelers

Woman Traveling
Traveling Tips
Planes-Ships-Trains
Traveling Tips Maintaining awareness
Selecting a secure Hotel
Check-in room rules
Taxis-Cars
Cars and Carjacking
Getting out Of Your Car
Vehicle Safety tips
Valet parking
Carjackers Places
The bank

Chapter 3...112

Home Invasion-Home safety
Daytime break-ins
Dangerous Home Situation
Existent weapons in a home
Safeguard your home in
Google Map
Home Security Tactics
Placing an emergency call
Outside Safety tips
Public Transportation

Self-defense techniques
True Equalizer a Gun
Self-defense Lessons
Strike chart 1-2-3-4
Where and how to strike
Defense Tips
In the Ultimate Moment
Sudden Weapons
Simple weapons

Chapter 4…………………………………………….. 157

Jogging, Biking, walking the
dog
Running Awareness
Self-defense definition
Stand Your Ground, Duty to
Retreat and Castle Doctrine.
Preventing Strategies

Keep up with the news
Facing the moment
Getting help
Weapons
Personal weapons
Street Smarts

Chapter 5...174

The predator, rapist
Rape-day drug
The Date Rape Drug of
Choice
Dept. of Justice data-2018
College rape
Sexual Violence-Times of
the Year
Preventing rape
Rape
What to do if- drugged and
raped
Sex Attacks

Red flags for a woman
Mistakes women make
Notes for woman
Walking or jogging
Tips Defense
Women's self-defense
College campus
Sorority/Fraternity
Sexting/ Sextortion
Men's fraternities
Common mistakes women
make

Chapter 6...209

Purse snatching
Protecting Children
Kids Internet Safety
Lessen your chances of being
a victim
Cane defense
Self Defense Tactics for
Women

Make awareness part of your
life
Awareness in your car
Phone Precautions
Tips on the street
Keep in mind thoughts
Canine attacks

Chapter 7...234

Identity theft
How does credit card get
stolen?
Phones rip-offs on the elderly
Medical Identity Theft
Mass Shooting surviving
Terrorist/ Terrorism
Chemical Attack
Hostage situations

Personal Security
Terrorism at workplace
Lone Wolf
Workplace violence, assaults
Flash-mob Riot
Hijacking
The New Cyber Assault
Cyberbullying
Safety Tips in Cyberspace

Chapter 8...269

Final thoughts
Conclusion of violent
consequences
Tips to help protect you, your
loved ones
Putting it all together
About the Author

Memory lane-Author Pictures
Knowledge Wordlists
Photo Credit
Gras Publishing Present
Protector
Sergio Oliva the Myth
El Atentado del Siglo

Chapter 1-Introduction Knowledge is power!!

This book's goal is not to teach you to fight, but to learn how to prevent an attack by being alert of the danger signs before the attack take place. The earlier you detect a potential problem, the more options you have to resolve it.

That's why I wrote this book, I want to take you step by step through a course of action that will transform your habits for the rest of your life and keep you and your family safe for decades to come.

These strategies and actions are basic, easy to learn and proven effective under stress, but it also teaches you basic attack moves in case it comes to defend yourself. Streetwise Extreme Surviving the Unexpected is basic for individuals who don't have previous training, or desire not to get one.

This book covers home invasion, terrorist attack, rape, Date Rape Drugs, driving safety, abroad safety, ATM safety, weaponless defense, improvised weapons, firearms, safety at home, Cyber-safety, Identity theft, Canine Attacks, and child safety. Also, it teaches you experience tips to learn how carjackers, muggers, rapists, junkies operates- and how to avoid them and much more.

This is an approach intended to defuse real-life violence. Focusing on street-oriented techniques, learn how to be aware and prevent violence, and de-escalate possible aggressive encounters

You will learn what works work for you, what doesn't, and then modified it to you, according to your age, strength, ability, skill, and fitness. Effective world practices that I have proven on the streets, and extreme locations in many parts of the world.

Perceive an ambushing situation? Prevent getting sucker punched? Discover tips on bullies, weapons, also covers unarmed self-defense, improvised weapons, firearms, rape, rape attempt is one of the most horrendous assaults a woman can experience, and teaches you a series of street-realistic techniques based on what real sexual predators do to make woman victim, and much more.

The reality is that the best defense is not having to fight at all, walk away unharmed, to your home or family.

The author reveals demonstrated approaches that facilitate you confront a life-threatening situation, immediately de-escalating possible confrontations and preventing would-be attackers.

He will not teach you how to become an expert fighter. It will show you how to prevent an attack by being aware of the danger signs that precede one. Plus, learn how important is your attitudes and actions, how to warn thugs that you are not an easy target. Finally, some easy basic fighting techniques proven to be effectively if you ever get to need them.

You will learn the skills, and ability to survive a violent confrontation. Whether that means being able to escape, or stop your opponent. You will learn how to: use proven awareness techniques for avoiding most confrontations; improve fighting skills; and maximize mental toughness

This book is based on differing's types of sources, including interviews supplied by students on the wrong side of the law as well as personal experiences from years past , and visiting and traveling questionable neighborhoods and cities. Professionally, I have experience teaching and working with at-risk youth for over 30 years. I wanted to help young men get out of gangs, and pick the right social way. I did times after time.

I was in a flash political riot in Bolivia and in a student march in the city of La Paz, Bolivia, also in a flash political riot in Mexico City when visiting the Mexico City University.

Some cities I have visited, driven and walked through the streets; many are the most dangerous cities in the USA and abroad. Later in the book in the travelers' chapter you will find more about specific dangerous neighborhoods I have visited, which I believe helped me shape my awareness, alert program.

This method requires no training or experience at all, no matter of size, gender, age, or strength. It is designed to quickly maximize your ability to survive criminal violence. Try out this simple, flexible protection approach so you are ready to counterattack a surprise lethal assault.

Violence against harmless people occur anytime, anywhere, especially to woman, older folks and teenagers throughout the world. The real objective of this book is to understand the knowledge to avoid violence, before it happens. This is critical!!

We live in the USA a free nation with laws, It is easy for people to think that living in the United States is safe, but in reality an attack could happen to anybody anywhere. People always tell me when I teach them about being aware that they don't want to, live in a world where they have to constantly be looking for danger. I always reply, you could enjoy life and learn to be always alert without being any paranoid. Staying alert is not becoming paranoid, it is being aware of your surroundings.

I demonstrate how to turn everyday objects into weapons or unarmed skills and techniques to defend you. The object of this book is to teach you how to avoid a dangerous situation, but if you have to, surprise the attacker before he has the opportunity to strike.

Most of the lesson I learned growing up and living in Miami, FL. Also, I have visited many sites and dangerous places and learned from them.

Several of the things I learned as a teenager walking down a dark street. Many times I came running to my front doorsteps with a bunch youth gang members in my tail right to my home front door. I've been in many fights, by myself and gangs related.

The Author Younger years

I've had my wrist broken three times (the boxer fracture), I had shoulder separations twice, and broken toes and broken bones from fights and training.

I used to keep a look for any potential improvised weapon and escape routes, and continue to do so today.

Most of all, I think the greatest gift that I retained from growing up and living with some required effort to stay safe was learning to stay ready, to be prepared to act if something bad happened. Growing up in an aggressive area I realized fast that you have to stand up for yourself. I adopted several tactics I learned from my youth days, and I still practice them every day. Much of this book's advice is also from talks with offenders. They focus on simplicity and effectiveness. A lot of it still comes from the days when I was in Junior High and came running home because a gang of teens were following me to beat me even to my front home door. My friends and I had to regroup, hang together, visit the school bathroom with a friend, never by yourself, many times we had to stay one hour after school was over, hiding so we could leave school grounds because gangs were waiting for us in any corner.

I remember we had to steal the forks and knives from school lunch, metal at that time, so we could have weapons. We were two or three skinny guys, and the gangs were 10 or 12 guys. Much bigger and stronger than us, many of them were from High School, even Football players. It was a very rough time for me and for some of my friends.

I began taking Japanese Karate, Okinawa when I was 13 years old, months later I found it was not appropriate for me, then I took Chinese Wing Chun Kung-Fu for many years, my father who was an amateur boxer in his youth taught me how to box, then I mixed and took from them what worked for me, I have trained this way for most of my life.

Vigilance and prevention are the foundation on which I have written this book. This isn't a martial arts book. This book does not expect you to learn difficult moves or specific skills; just simple, practical, precise, but basic effective moves. You don't need fancy equipment or practice for long hours every day.

The Author Frank Marchante

16

You will learn how to survive a critical encounter, but most importantly how to avoid it entirely by de-escalating an imminent attack.

Even if you never do exercise, this book, the information contained within its pages could save your life, and the life of your loved one. Self-defense for no aggressive people: Protect yourself, no matter size, gender, age, or strength. Being safe is more than practicing self-defense, or practicing shooting. You're reading this book because you want to learn and take steps to ensure not only your own safety, but also your family.

The victims I've spoken always have neglected most of the safety rules. If you think ahead, before it happens, what you would do if this happens to me here or there? Then, you will be ahead of the assailant. I assure you, you will surprise the aggressor and probably he will look for another victim. Prevention is Knowledge, Knowledge is power.

Most people think that self-defense is training to strike, and kick. I believe self-defense, it is about reeducation the mind to acknowledge threats and how to respond: should you fight back when attacked, or run, and scream or talk your way out of a beating, consent to handing your money, giving up your car, or when to drive through a mob and speed off.

Honesty is the first chapter in the book of wisdom.
Thomas Jefferson

Street Wise Extreme

Have you ever felt scared or intimidated when are out walking alone? What would you do if threatened by an attacker?

The truth

This book offers practical and down to earth advice on personal safety for both men and woman. Unlike most self-defense or martial arts book, this book is focused in practical, real life violence situation; it is not aiming for sport or competition. The techniques that I disclosure here for you to learn are very simple and effective, nothing confusing, or extremely hard to. Especially for ordinary people. Woman or men just like you and me.

Author High School years

This book will not teach you to become a fighter or a champion, self-defense is about preventing, ending a violent attack, unharmed, and escaping out of danger as fast as you can. That's what self-defense really is. Easy to say, Right? However, very hard to do. If it was that easy you just won't be reading this book right now.

Based on the hundreds of individual hours I have coached and spoken with many bullies, predators and people on the wrong side of the Law I came up with an approach that you can follow to accomplish the goal of self-defense in the streets. After 30 years of teaching, advocating for survival readiness, I included about every survival-related subject there is. My goal was introduced to you, ideas in an easy-to-read format. That will help the reader understand and learn awareness and self-defense skills

Author teaching

I'm not claiming to be a champion or an expert fighter, I'm not, but I will teach you Survival Lessons learned from experiences walking thru the Streets of La Paz, Bolivia, Peru, Ecuador, Mexico City, Dominican Republic New York, California, New Orleans, Philadelphia, Miami, FL and other cities. This book teaches you tips for security in the streets. Feel safe at home. Develop the street smarts instinct, security when traveling to other countries, and how to stay always ahead of the predator or criminal actions.

This book is based on escape **awareness.** The self- defense tactics, and strategies taught in this book have been successfully employed by women, man, old, weak people, youngsters, and by me.

Self-defense Techniques must be simple to be useful under pressure and under any circumstances.

This book gives woman of all ages and sizes Rape Awareness and Prevention -how to recognize before the attack is delivery and defend against each, just by following these tips you will be safer. The tips and techniques in this book could easily be the difference between life and death in a dangerous situation. This book is not based as a sport, or for a champion, or to make you one, it is intended to counter street violence, avoiding, escaping, and as if you have to fight, survive

For a man and the young you don't have to be a fighter or a martial art expert to be able to use these techniques.

For the older this book will give you tactics and techniques, which any common woman or man can archives, people like you and me. The purpose of this book is to help overcome personal powerlessness.

Self-defense means:

A- Awareness   D- Mental Preparedness
B- Prevention   F- Tactics, Skills
C- Escaping routes   G- Fighting

Defusing different lethal situations with verbal techniques.
If you must defend yourself.

Less tactics are better. Which one is the best?
Which tactic to use if you are weak, small woman or you do not practice martial art or any defense arts.

The majority of self-defense instructors think that you need many different self-defense skills so you can use in the streets to protect yourself. I think it is the other way around. If you learn well one or two fighting skills, you can repeat them over and over with accuracy.

If you are baby boomers you must realize and get ready for a world that is changing fast every day. The world is becoming more and more dangerous. You only have to watch the 11:00pm TV news to know.

How to effectively deal with the most common attacks against women!
Not this book or a hundred books can teach you to survive a 100 % on the street—each street person's situation is unique. However, this book will give tips in street survival that worked.

A motive

A motive which gave me the idea to do this book was the increasing problem in this growing society of crimes, home invasion and the likes. Base thru personal experience I acquire living thru during the 1960s very turbulent time when I joined a fraternity or gang called "45" because we were 45 guys. Some of my group went on to become lawyers, teachers and even doctors. Some took or stayed on the wrong side of the law and are dead now, or jailed doing 30 years or life sentence for various hard crimes.

Frank Marchante

Professionally, I had experience teaching and working with at-risk youth for over 30 years in a public school. I wanted to help young men get out of gangs, and pick the right social way. I did times over time. Those youth provided me with many valuable hints. Here again some of my students went on to become lawyers, teachers and doctors too.
Many went the wrong way, despite the many long hours of conversations I had with them trying to help them change their way of living. Unfortunately, this is the group I'm focusing on this book. I will mention some examples of some of them. The young men, who shot and killed a highway trooper on the freeway one night, and the bizarre story is that the trooper came to his aide because his car has

stall (stop) ,no, no drugs or alcohol was found on his body after the arrest a couple of hours later and test was done.

Another case is the leader of a car theft ring and home invasion, this gentleman use to brag that he could get into any car in less than 20 seconds and into a house in less than three minutes. I also remember the young lady who stood, between two rival gangs and said, if you are going to shoot my boyfriend you have to shoot thru me. That's what they did and kills her on the spot. Another case that comes to mind is a young man, Raul, who was shot in his head and killed while robbing a gas station. Another is doing life in prison after attending to rob a Well Fargo truck and things got out of hand and according to what he told me, he never intended to kill anybody, but the guard almost open fire on him and he had to shoot to save his own life.

And the last case example, I'm going to mention, of the many I could tell you about is a young man I will call here Carlos. He was a bright, strong and a nice looking young man, he got to hang around with the wrong croup, a group that was moving some kind of drugs. Despite the many times I spoke to him, he did not stop his sharing time with this gang. He gave me his word that he was not participating or trafficking any substance, I believe him then as much as I still do now. He was hanging with them because they allowed him to use nice cars and there has been always beautiful woman present.

Last time I went to talk to him because of his mother requested it from me, I always got a good rapport with all my students good or bad and they really felt at ease with me as much as a felt at ease with them. I went to this apartment where he agreed to see me. We spoke for about an hour, he promised me that he will no longer hang around with this group because of his mother worries.

The Author Teaching

That night, another group surprises everybody in that apartment and shoot everybody's death, including my student who was present. This situation still haunts me after so many years, I almost save his life, but

21

did not. I could have been shot and killed too when the shooting took place, remember I was in that apartment less than 10 hours before. That's why I respect teachers more than any other professionals, they go out of their way and do things that the school boards never knows and if they were to find out I doubt it very much will care.
Spending 30 years with all kinds of people, different nationalities, races and backgrounds and talking hundreds of hours , listening to their conversations , I learned what make them tick, how they react, think, what and how they pick a victim, etc.

I'm surprised when I see somebody in a dangerous situation and I made comments about it to the person with me at the time. They looked at me like saying, What? What are you talking about?

It's like they are blind or I have x vision, they do not see or realize what I'm talking about.
They don't understand and I know why, because they were never exposed to the people or situation I have.

That's also why the people I see are doing or allowing themselves into a situation that makes them an easy target or a victim.

No one has the right to take advantage of another simply because is a woman, a small man, a weak or old man or a child.

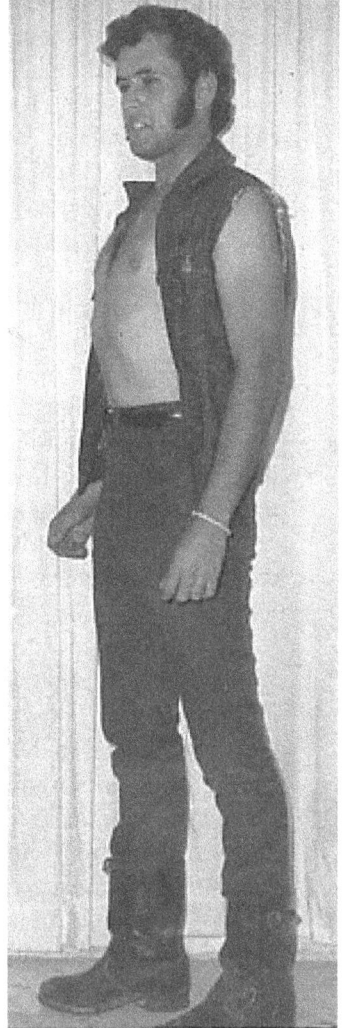

The Author younger year

Defensive Awareness

The most important step you must learn to increase your ability to remain safe is **AWARENESS**. By being aware, you can avoid most frightening situations. Awareness is the ability to **"read"** situations and anticipate violent attacks before it happens. It is knowing what to look for.

Street smarts

Street smart means somebody with excellent common sense. These individuals possess a skill to function on the streets, someone who knows when to avoid potentially negative situations. They also know who can they trust, and how to handle themselves in bad areas of town. This knowledge they have not learned from a book/school. They have learned in the streets.

This book is ideal for anyone who wants to learn to survive in the streets of today.

You don't need martial arts to defend yourself. Or be a champion fighter. Awareness is the trick.

You must learn: passive and aggressive strategy, planned De-escalation tactics, awareness, hand placement for defense, escaping tips, recognize the cues of physical violence, and to fight if you must. You will learn what to do and how to keep your eyes open in this scenario. Contains pictures, to illustrate some points.

Awareness without action is worthless.
Phil Mcgraw

Attacks-Street Smart

Experts claim that awareness makes up 90% of self-defense the remaining 10% is physical and shape. When you are alert, you identify and can avoid dangerous situations.

Self-defense practice and tactics must be fast and to the point, with no wasting time. Also, must represent the least amount of danger for the person being attacked or defending himself
Fear gives the advantage over his victim.
Rapist and criminals are looking for an easy target.

Street safe

For you to survive a street fight, forget those elaborate cools move you have seen in the movies they simply will not work. Period, it's very easy in a karate school or Judo for you to handle your partner, I respect every Martial Arts Style, the schools, the teachers and the people who practice hours after hours. Many great fighters come out of those schools, I'm sure.

For years I was a believer in the martial arts for defense. As a matter of fact, in my younger years I took some kung-Fu, some Karate and I practice some boxing because my father uses to box when he was young. I adjusted what came easy for me from these three styles and stick with them for years. Then, I was a witness of two incidents that made me change my way of thinking about it.

One time I personally saw a brawl between a black belt Karate instructor, which by the way was very good at his sport, face a fat man who probably overweight him 150 lbs easy. The fat men rush toward him like a bull , in three or four seconds the karate expert was out lying on the floor with three broken ribs, this was not a surprise fight , both were facing each other and knew they were about to fight.

The other time as a teacher one of my students was my state teenager Karate champion for two years in a row, again, I witness a brawl fight between this champion and a guy about the same high and weight, the other guy was a regular young guy and he was a street fighter, no style, no form, no discipline whatsoever. To my surprise the street fighter won the fight with wild punches, pushing and bulling the

24

champion, it was over in minutes. Again, this young champion was very, very good in his art.

I learned that the Martial Arts are perfect for sport and getting in shape, but questionable for self- defense in a real life or death situation, at least in a regular person, who is not a champion.

A predator attack is fast and vicious; this is why it ensures their victory. This makes the street thug predictable. There are many danger signs that you must learn to avoid the criminal attacks. This book will open your mind to think like a predator, you must learn to think like one and learn to read those signs so you can prevent the criminal from launching his attack on you.

There are no conciliators in a street fight!

Self-defense to be useful does not have to require physical peak, top fitness level or maximum flexibility. Self-defense has to be affordable no matter your condition, age, size; otherwise it would not be practical.

Self-defense must be useful for the frail person, and for the poorly coordinated person. Of course the same technique will be more effective if the person is in better shape. No matter how small or weak a person may be, he/she has the ability to use his body in a life or death situation, in other words to defend himself.
Take from this book what is useful to you and the situations you think you may fall into one day, discard the rest.

To survive in a street situation you have to learn how to think like a Predator. You have to be able to foresee who is likely to ambush you, attack, try to rape you or robbed you.
Knowledge, awareness, proper behavior and the ability to recognize the dangerous situation on the spot, fast without thinking, just like a reflex or like you breathe. True Self-defense becomes a skill, when you applied these behaviors to your lifestyle.
Staying safe from predators and violence doesn't require much from you, you must acquire some habits and modify your behavior.

Forget pride, emotions and anger, when it comes to saving your life or the life of somebody you love and care.
For real self-defense, there is no need to spend years in martial arts schools.

25

Don't forget

Self-defense is not allowing yourself to get into in a danger situation
The best self-defense technique is to run, escape out of dangerous
ways.
We use her or he thought the book to describe the target, the recipient
and the predator or criminal.

Vale Incident

A friend of mine and his wife, were out shopping, and just cashed a
check at 4:00 pm in the afternoon in a newly developed food
shopping center, while approaching theirs vehicle, a man drove up
beside them, coming in the other direction they were walking, to ask
for directions. As my friend came in close to the car to answer, the
man reached out of his window and pointed a gun at my friend's face,
one or two feet from him, demanded his wallet and the cash from the
check he just had cashed.

The thief was probably disappointed when he discovered only one
hundred dollars cash in his wallet, including the check cashed.
Everything indicates the thief was working with somebody in the
store to know he just cashed the check. My friend could have
prevented the crime just if he had been aware.

Had he scanned the parking lot as they walked to their car, the
suspicious car coming around for a second time thru the parking lot
would have been spotted. He remembers the car passing once next to
them, going around so the driver could be facing him as they walked
to their car.

My friend and his wife should have changed lines, from the side they
were walking to the one on the other side of the parked cars, and as
the car came around for another time, again move themselves to the
other side. Bet you anything that this action would have dissuaded the
robber, to look for another victim, the factor surprise being a thief's
best weapon, it would have been lost.

This book will give you the basics you will need to win a physical
confrontation or better yet, see it develop before it happens.

These individuals have no major respect for person or property. Criminals, view their world through the eyes of a predator. Those whose waking hours are filled with the thought, who has got what I want, that I can take from them? You know the kind I'm talking about.

We all secretly hope that we will never cross paths with this type of felons. However, unfortunately, which is not going to prevent a run in with these types.

"Gut instinct." Avoid a person or a situation which does not "feel" safe.

More than one person attack

A **group** attack is something to really fear. You can be killed, or you will get hurt bad. To survive you have to be prepared. You must Stop the attack, create confusion and make as much noise as you can.

One common description of a **gang** is a group of three or more individuals who act together in criminal activity and identify themselves with a common name or sign.
There is no time to waste, in this unfair situation; if you hesitate you will lose, period. So, don't waste time. Every second that passes your chances of getting out get smaller.

They are going to intimidate you, mentally dictate the situation, using fear of course. They are going to push you a couple of times first to disorient you.
If you act forcefully and fast against your attackers, you turn the surprise fact to them. Remember, they do not want a confrontation or a fight, just a victim or an easy prey.
Gangs are strong and powerful together, when they are together that makes them mentally strong and will do things that probably by themselves won't do.

Avoid if possible

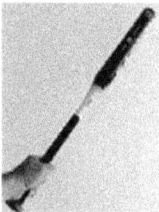

If you see a gang in the street on your way, go across the street, get in a store or fast food for a couple of minutes till they pass, some people tells me when I tell them to do this action, they said I live in the USA, the most powerful country, we have laws, why I have to cross the street if that's not where I'm going?.
I know and they have a point in this way of thinking, but do you really think the gangs care? Do you really think you could walk by them in the daytime, even worst at night, without being harass, name calling, provoke, touch if you are a woman, or molested, robbed, or hurt. If you do, then you are dreaming.

Because I'll bet you anything that you won't walk through them without any problems. The best action is to avoid them, it makes takes only a few minutes, believe me it is not worth it.

In my late teenage years, one day I walked out of a building to find out that my motorcycle was surrounded by a gang of about twenty or twenty five guys. I did something very stupid and I was very lucky. I could tell about ¼ of a block from them that they had some kinds of Bamboo stick or what maybe looked like sugar cane, I don't know, but it was like a foot or one and a half feet long.

I kept walking to them, when I reach them I picked an empty soda glass bottle from the ground , hit the ground with it and broke it and kept the1/2 tip making it a weapon, when I got to them before they even said anything I yelled , go head , do it, I'm going to take one guy, just one, the first one that attacks me, right away before they even had a chance to answer , I yelled again, tonight when my people find out what happened to me they are going to go after you guys and I'll bet you they are going to get some of you alone and about ten or more are going to spend the night in the hospital. I kept yelling go ahead, I want one to take with me and about tonight when my friends find out.

I was really convinced that I was going to take one with me that I must have intimidated them. Did I scare them? No way, did I intimidate them? Maybe. For weeks after the incident, I was still sure that I could have taken one.

My yelling probably helped me. So all of a sudden the guy who seems the leader and much later I found out he was, said let's get out of here and leave this piece of shit. They walked away! The situation lasted about five minutes.

I was lucky because I did not get hurt, probably they thought, this guy is becoming a problem, what if he is saying it's true, let's leave and look for another victim that is not going to bring us that kind of problem, an easy prey. I was stupid because the action I should have taken was get back in the building ,call some friends to pick me up, call the police , or just wait around for them to get tired of waiting and leave. I recognize that, but when I was in my teens or twenties, I couldn't do it. Today that I'm mature is different, I comprehend and realize it. You have to be mature to understand this and try to lessen the situation.

The truth of the matter is that looking back now; I doubted very much that I could have taken one of them. However, my ego got in the way, how could I face my guys later? Anyway, my prestigious in my gang grew a couple of notches up. Also I heard that with that gang too, I got more respect from both of those groups.

De-escalation the situation

Another anecdote is, one day I was at the beach a few feet's away from the ocean getting a tan. All of a sudden a beautiful girl walked by me in a blue bikini, and I made a comment, nothing bad, something like whoop!! Or similar. When I see she keeps walking and join a group gang of guys , very tough bad looking guys, they all were very strong and nasty looking. All of a sudden about ten or so started walking my way.

I recognized the gang and the leader; I knew about them, this was the most notorious gang in my state with affiliates in many other states. As a gang, they were huge and really bad.

Again by the time they reach me, I stood up and before they had a chance to say or do anything I told the leader, who had also a blue swimming trunk, I thought you were a movie star or a famous actor, for a moment I thought you were Arnold Schwarzenegger with your bodyguards. I added, with that kind of muscle body you should be a star like Arnold or Jean Claude Van Damme. He stoped, looked at his body for a second, smile and then looked at his people who were in shock, I could see it in their eyes.

I had lifted his ego, but not only that, I did it in front of his peers, and I was not the enemy anymore. He was interested in what I had to say, so I kept talking about movies, exercises and so on. All of a sudden he signals his friends to move back to the beach. He stayed and we talked about ten or fifteen more minutes.

Then he left, but as he was leaving, he said, you like my girlfriend? Isn't she pretty?

To what I answered him, she is beautiful, you are very lucky, he laughed very loud and left. After talking to this guy, I could tell he was some kind of nice guy after all. The last time I heard of him he was doing ten to fifteen years jail time.

Would I try this technique again in my life? Maybe. Would it work again, who knows? It saved me that day.

This is what is called De-escalation the situation.

I make a point of always seating on the outside of a restaurant booth, the same for a movie theater, auditorium, or church. I also never sit with my back to the entrance door. I do this automatically without thinking and I've been doing it for the last 48 years. Why? Let me explain, once I was in a Sambo's restaurant, at the corner of 2690 W. Flagler Street, just one block from my high school, Miami Senior High with a bunch of friends, about eight of them. We sat in the back corner in a big booth. I was all the way inside the booth and I had a couple of girls on both sides.

A huge brawl occurred in the restaurant, things were thrown, I was trapped inside the booth and the girls next to me were ducking. I had a hard time getting out of the center of the booth and I had to drag myself over the food and glasses of water that were on the table. It was frightening. I've never forgotten the incident. There were about 10 police cars on the scene, including two tough officers that we used to call Batman and Robin. I ask you to do the same; try to always sit in the outside corner of the row of the Movie Theater, church, or restaurant booth. Also, face the entrance so you can see if someone enters the place with bad intentions. Once you get used to doing it, it's easy.

Use anything available

If you must fight use anything in your reach to defend yourself, tables, chairs, etc. And if you can, get an attacker to talk by making him think, you have slowed his response. You have also bought yourself some time to think, escape or for someone to get to you and maybe help you, seconds could be your salvation.

Don't become an easy target, become unpredictable.
Keep your balance and prevent with everything in your power been dropped to the floor.

Be aware of what is happening around you.

Yell, call for someone, make-believe name, make them think you are spec ting someone closed by to show or yell for the police, or use some tactic to that effect. Real or not you may confuse them and make the attack shorter.

Go for the leader

First, go for the leader, or of course the first person who attacks you, going after the leader is also a psychological trick. It's always to your advantage if possible for you to go after the leader, this will surprise the group and think of you much tougher than you really are.

I'm not going to lie and tell you, like many karate or self defense books to kick here, punch here, the truth is, your chances of getting alive from this situation or really hurt them is minimal. You should have never allowed yourself to be in this situation. I'm going to give you some tips, but like I said your chances are minimal.

First use your whole body to defend yourself, yell, make noises, call for an imaginary friend, call for the police, yell fire, anything to make noise and make a commotion.

You can also create confusion, move a lot if you can, push, shaved, Scratch or punch into the person who grabbed you, use a head butt, strike or elbow. Try to move to a much lighter area and busy street, into a store or building. If a car passes by signal it anything to call attention and to move you closer to where there is car traffic or people.

Maybe somebody will help you or at least call the police.

Use your head, shoulders, elbows, forearms, hands/fists, hips, knees, shins, and feet. Anything you can use. Bite someone ear, neck, arms, areas of the face, the throat, testicles, etc., anything goes. It is now or never.

32

Much smarter and intelligent is not to ever get in a situation like this. You must do whatever it takes to get out of this situation. I repeat whatever it takes to get out of this situation.

If you are thrown to the ground position your head toward your chest, cover the head and face with your arms to protect yourself as much as possible and yell as much as you can.
Yell things like, over here, police; keep protecting your head and vital organs while yelling as loud as you can.
Because if you don't, here are some list of the consequences.

1 You will get hurt
2 The Police won't be there to help

Your goal is to survive and escape as fast as you can

If you understand into the situation that there is no way out, but to fight, keep your mouth closed with your teeth squeeze, if your mouth is open you are looking to get your jaw broken.

Pay attention, find out and Circle away from his power side (go around to your right if he has his right hand angle back, go around to your left if he has his left hand angle back).

You need to keep at least two arms range or more away from him outside of his punching or kicking range.

Use your strongest weapons against his weakest targets. Don't try swapping punches with him; if you try to trade punches with him, you're probably playing right into his game.

Only as a last resort fight with your attacker. He is used to get into this kind of situation and probably he is going to hurt you. **Defend yourself only if you have to!**

Get a barrier between you and him even if you have to run around a car, tables or trees. Yell for help. You can't count on people coming to your aide, but he might think you know someone who will render assistance. Make your escape retreat and escape.

Move

The best way not to get hit badly is to move, always move.
Move off to an angle, or even better move in a circle. There are many people with different approach to this. The debate is which initial movements are better. The important key is to move out of the reach of punches. If you are standing, you have to move your feet to get out of reach. If you are thrown on the ground, make sure to move your hips even if you can't move anything else to be off line, making a little harder to be hit straight in the face.

The huge advantages of moving is to make yourself a harder target to hit. You force him to make an extra movement to get to you. You change the complete reality of the moment.

When you move that gives you the opportunity to get into a better advantageous position, delay the confrontation time and maybe it is enough for someone to step in ,come by, even the police, believe me if you gain ¼ of a minute that is great .

Never, never allow your opponent to make a series of moves without answering or countering any of them, otherwise you are going to be hit and hard.

So the best defense you can have is to move. Your movement will make his fighting least effective.
First, you should step back and at the same time step back at an angle. Remember back and in an angle, very important.

If you move straight back, although better than nothing the attacker can gain ground faster? Better to step back at an angle. Often, it's even better to step off at a right angle.

Professional studies demonstrated that most attacks are likely to escalate into homicides when there is more than one attacker, particularly when the attackers are youngsters.

Try to maneuver attackers into a single line so they cannot all hit you at the same time. Move, I repeat, move don't be a sitting target and try to breach their line so you can get out.

The way multiple attackers work is, one attacker, usually the one facing and threatening you, will keep your attention while the others attack from your blind side, like the back or side. If you sense an attack is about to happen and there is no way out, attack first. This is the most dangerous factor in such a scenario all experts agree to. I know it is something very hard to do, but you must do it.

A strategy expert said they have used in the past is trying to make the group choose a leader to fight. Tell the guy, "Do you want to fight? You and me, one-on-one. Do you need all of these guys to help you right? Then, point to the crowd. Now his honor is at stake, you place him in a very difficult position in front of his gang. He can't admit that he needs help. This will not work a 100% in all circumstances, but has work for some in the past. What would you gain? Well, is better to fight one guy even if he beat you than to be beaten by 10 guys. Don't you agree? I personally don't believe it; sooner or later they all are going to jump in. Give it a try if you think will help you.

If there are people present beside the guys from the gang, for public safety it is often effective to ask, "Do you want to go to jail?"

Don't threaten them never ever. Don't give away the element of surprise. Don't jump into a fighting pose; if you do, you've given the group time to think about what their response will be. Non-telegraphic movement. The surprise for self-defense is priced less.

Never ever allowed to be encircled

Try to move as much as you can try to keep your body with one crook between you and the others. I know that famous experts recommend keeping your back against the wall, a technique that I have used in the past usefully, but now I have doubts about it.

Always attack or defend yourself to the one closest to you, better yet the one who is blocking the escape route or the one who is the most direct threat. Don't waste time if this situation ever happens, you must strike fast, hard to do the most damage you are capable of. Never turn your back to an assailant even if the confrontation or fight you **think** is over. Do not overlook anyone, and don't try to reason with a vicious criminal or rapist, ever!

Always move

Observable Threat

Immediately Threat

If a man/ group is walking toward you, insulting you and take out any weapon. There are no doubts about their objective.

Not direct Threat

He looks like an average man, but he is looking kind of nervous at you, he seems agitated and he is kind of walking in your way.

Unlikely Threat

Most of the time you won't see a sign that danger is coming your way and the most danger is that the attack will be a shock.

Tips

If anyone refuses to make eye contact, this could mean danger.
If he or they are blinking excessively this is considerate a sign of nervousness. Be careful.

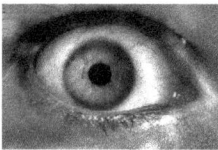

A person with eyes wide open, this is a sign of a dangerous aggressive person. Stay alert.

If the eyes are fixed in you, this is common of violent people that intend to use violence against you. Get ready.

Someone with the eyes glassy it could means he is under some kind of drug, alcohol, a sign to keep you alert because he might be thinking in getting some money for his habits. From you!!

Notice also the voice, if he/they are yelling at you with profanity, the attack could be imminent. Take necessary steps to avoid it. Keep some distance so you don't get sucked punch.

Alert

When you read, a magazine or a smart phone, don't wear earplugs listening to music. You need to hear if somebody is approaching, keep your head high, keep your reading matter to your eye level. This will let you perceive any imminent danger.

Victims always said the attacker came from nowhere. The victim did not perceive or hear the attacker. If you recognize the attack is just about to happen, you can get ready to fight, run, yelled or fly. The truth is, that is not in some people's nature to fight.

Getaway
Very important is finding where you move if there is trouble. Most mass murders enter through the front door. Robbers always hit the cashier stand nears the front door. Always keep this in mind, if you are shopping especially at night.

Lights
Criminal like darkness. A good idea is to have illumination, in case your key falls down. Smartphones have lights, even a small flashlight, or a key chain with a light is great to have.

Travel
Check travel routes with the internet before you go, check hotels and destinations .John Farnam a retired marine officer used to say, "avoid the three stupid", "don't go to stupid places", or "do stupid things with stupid people."

Improvised defense weapons.
A pen tip, water bottle, belt, a lamp, a phone, a flashlight can also be used for self-defense. If you don't have a weapon, you can improvise one.

Personal alarm
While walking to your car, hold your car key alarm in your hands, if you need to you may press the panic button. Maintain it by your bed at night, if you push the panic button late at night you can confuse the intruder, giving you time to hide, escape, he most likely runs away because of the noise and surprise of what is happening.

Men Surprise Attacks

Troubles can many times find you and any men should recognize that at any time or place now a day anybody can be a victim. Even when minding your own and never looking for any problem. The Problem can find you and look you in the eyes at any moment in time

You must anticipate and be ready for all kinds of attack. If you are

seated having dinner with a girlfriend or a friend and someone approaches you and throw a punch at you. What would you do? Which way would you react? Are you going to have time to face this attacker or is he going to sucker punch you? This is the kind of situation you have to think in your mind before it happens. In your mind tell yourself if this happens to me, this

and that is what I'm going to do. I would kick him from my seat, or I would throw him in the face my drink, giving me a few seconds to stand up to this man.

If you take the subway or the bus, run thru your mind various scenarios so if it ever happens your mind already has a way to cope with it. What about if you are using the bathroom in a public place. How would you react? One day think about all the situations you may face one day and in your mind find the way out or the way you would like to react.

Think of many different scenarios and places, what about if your attacker is drunk or high on some kinds of drugs. Think how you would like to handle a situation like that.

This is a tremendous exercise in safety; you come to your action plan in your mind three or four times or even more. Believe if it ever happens, you have a better chance to get out unharmed because of your mind predisposition to your plan.

Anticipate all kinds of attacks

You have different kinds of criminals

The hardened criminal-Very dangerous, kills for any reason whatsoever.

Gangs- found in bad neighborhoods, looking for easy victims, to steal and destroy properties.

Addict- a criminal to support his habit, if needs to kill for drugs, be it.

Drug user-are under the influence of drugs, crazy maniacs, inflicts pain for pleasure.

The juvenile- wants easy money for drugs or gadgets. Breaking in your house; steal a wallet or purse, anything for a couple of dollars.

The crazy-hurt, torture or kill for satisfaction.

Robbery is the offense of seizing **property** through aggression or **intimidation**. In streets words, robbery is defined as taking the property of another.

In a real attack situation the assault is over in few shorts minutes or seconds, seconds are filled with panic and chaos, and you won't have time to think clearly.

You must decide very fast your action plan, are you going to try to escape, run, hire, call somebody or are going to fight back. Seconds count, make your decision and go for it.

Murder begins where self-defense ends.
Georg Buchner

39

Street Tactics Awareness

The clothes you are wearing, the people you are with, the way you talk or move it is all very important in a confrontational situation. Learn how to avoid a fight, get out and escape or what to do when you can't.

By being aware or alert to your surrounding you can avoid most threatening situations. To explain the levels of awareness, I would like to use the **color code system** learned from Colonel Jeff Cooper, a famous self –defense gun expert and writer, founder of the Gun-site Academy tactical shooting school. Used by most military and police organizations, to differentiate different levels of awareness.

He codified his color code so people understood the mental move that takes to go from unaware to ready to shoot or react.

Color Code System

White: Totally unaware. Home reading, watching TV, with doors and windows closed.

Yellow: Aware of what is going on. Not scare, just paying attention. Observing what is going on around you.

Orange: Understanding something is not right. The parking lot is very dark, is was not full as when you got in, a couple of strange looking guys are standing in a corner looking at you, and starting to walk your way. Pay much closer attention.

Red: you know something is wrong. You are in danger. Red is time to act! Escape or fight. If you have the option to escape to a safe place much better. **Get out now!**

Using these levels of awareness will help you avoid becoming a victim of violent crime, just as they have helped me since I learn to use the color system.

Staying alert is not becoming paranoid, it is being aware of your surroundings.

Think about this for a moment!

Most situations can be avoided and de-escalated. Two mad people get into a discussion and out of the blue there is the famous dare, "Let's take it outside!" If you go out understand that you or the other person it's going to get hurt, the police are going to come, somebody may get hurt, it could be you or maybe some arrest will take place.

Then remember, probably you will need to hire a lawyer, go to a trial for something minor that just intensify. Was it worth, it? No, was not. When my kids were smaller I just used to tell myself , don't do it , don't get in this stupid situation, leave the confrontation ,the problem for a real life situation where my kid's life or somebody like a family member was in real danger.

This way it would be acceptable to go thru all the problems, only and only in a really dangerous situation. Believe it or not that way of thinking kept me away of many incidents that otherwise would have escalated who's knows where.

By the way, you should read about the laws in your state and learn about self-defense and what the law said. It's always good to know and have the law, by your side.
What you do, talk and how you are saying it will affect the situation. How you act and talk will keep you out of most physical altercations, and that's what true self-defense is; keeping harm's way to a minimum.

Let me tell you about an incident that took place a couple of weeks back. I walked to a coffee shop window with my wife and daughter, there was a man standing by the window and for some reason he was taking all the window counter space, like if he was too big or the only person around. When I got close to him, I thought that he has been taken care already, I said excuse me and move close to the window by

his side. When the lady at the shop came over and said may I help you? Just in case I said, he was first so take care of him.
The man turns around and said of course I was first. Who do you think you are passing by my space? I responded, Sir, I said excuse me when I passed by you and even told the waitress that you were first. Now the waitress said, that's correct, he said that.

The man in a very nasty attitude said, yea, yea, yea, and make what I interpreted a very nasty gesture. I admit it, I lost it with this guy, I told my wife and daughter very loud, move out of the way I'm going to have to exchange blows with this guy. Right away I got into a semi-defensive stance and yelled at this guy, let's do it, let's exchange some blows, come on let's do it.

By now the guy took his coffee and left. As you can see I **escalated** the situation because so far the man never mentioned or intended to hit me. What about if the man went for it and we got into a fight. For something stupid like a cup of coffee? He or I could have gotten hurt. In front of the police probably it would have been my fault because I was the one who wanted to fight. Then, you heard this news on the TV news and you said how stupid a fight over coffee.

I admitted that was stupid from my side. However, for some reason I reacted like that. This is an example of escalating the situation.

If you escalate the situation, for example, some one punch you in the face and you take out a gun and shot him, that's escalating the situation and you very believe it you are going to be in some kind of trouble with the police.

If you ever get in a situation that you hurt someone really bad, when the police arrive, wait until you spoke to an attorney before making any kind of statement.

When you walk into a place, you must be able to recognize the bullies, predators from the family and average person just mining their ways.
The best ways to avoid being the victim of a predator is staying away from places that they frequents, dark streets, lonely corners, public bathrooms not well lighted, not close to people traffic , bars, etc.

Another example of being aware that I want to share to show you why many women or most people are surprised and assaulted.

About two weeks ago, my wife, daughter and I went to eat to a nice Coral Gables Miami, FL restaurant. This is one of the most prestigious or desire section in Miami, Fl.

After we finish eating, we decide to walk three blocks to a Barnes & Noble bookstore because it was still early, and we left the car park in the street by the Italian restaurant. We left the bookstore about 10:00 PM as we were approaching the corner where we were parked, I saw two men's very suspicious, wearing dark caps and rude looking for this part of town seating by the corner outside of a coffee shop that it was closed and the lights were out.

Right away I got alert, I could not cross the street because my car was parked 20 feet from these guys and all of the stores were close across the street anyway. I looked around and decided my options fast.

First of all I looked at them right in the eyes, not provoking, just letting them know I was aware. I change places with my daughter to be close to them in case they decide to make a move. Also, I move as I walked away from them as I could, to give me time to react if they did attack. I placed my hand in my pants pocket holding the car key, I did this for three reasons, first not to lose any time when I got to my car, use the keys for defense and also to make them think that I had a weapon or gun, with my other hand I grab my telephone in open view.

I passed them and we looked at each other for a few seconds, not starring I repeat, we go to the car I open the door and said fast everybody inside, my wife unaware of the situation started to talk , I interrupted her and I almost yelled, inside now fast. We all got in, started the car and got out not even waiting for the seatbelt to be worn.

My daughter was the first one to say, did you see those guys? And added I was worried and ready. My wife commented, which guys? I did not see anyone. See what I mean about being aware. If my wife had been alone or with a friend who acted just like her probably she or they had been robbed.

I decided a block away what to do if they have acted, at that time it was some traffic still, I would have given my phone to my daughter ready to call 911 and ask her to run, at the same time I have noticed a big empty wood box in the bus bench just inches from where I was going to walked by, I planned to throw it into the street to make cars stop and make a traffic commotion, then turn around and defend myself, moving, yelling, punching.

Hoping with the cars jammed call people's attention to the robbers so they will be worried and scare and run away, 90% better than to be taken by surprise. This is what criminals want. Surprise you.

I'm grateful that nothing happened, but I assure you that it was at least a scared moment.

The predator mind does not think like decent or working people. They era always thinking opportunities, if you make a wrong move, a mistake they will strike, you could be relaxing for example, at the beach with your family , but make no mistake close by is a predator waiting for your mistake. Or in parking lot, they are always in the looked out for victims mistake or an easy prey like most of them refer to their victims.

Most victims walked with their heads down, never make any eye contact, always keep their voices down. These are inviting sign for the predator or criminal.

I wish I could tell you how to distinguish the predator or bully, but I can't. In the movies, it's really easy, but in real life is not. The good dressed and one that articulates very nicely could be the criminal. Keep in mind he is not going to look suspicious; otherwise you are going to be on the lookout.

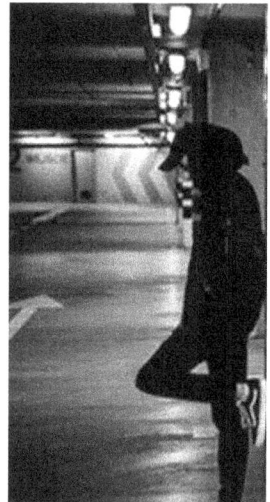

Remember, the bully or predator is looking for a victim and not a confrontation or an adversary.

Better to fight for something than live for nothing.
George S. Patton

Bullies

If you are facing a bully, the bully always uses verbal abuse. Like "What are you doing here?" or "What are you looking at?" Move let me pass or get out of my f... way or something similar. Bullies select targets to hurt.

He is a wild animal; likewise the criminal or predator wants an easy target. He will look for those he sees as flaccid, passive and probably not to fight back. He doesn't want a contender and he doesn't want to be getting hurt himself.

The predator is looking for a victim who is unaware, preoccupied, on the go, in a rush, someone who makes a mistake. If you are aware of your surroundings, you are increasing the chances of detecting and stopping a dangerous criminal.

On many occasions thugs ask you what time it is; don't look at your wristwatch, tell him a rough calculation without stooping and don't take your eyes away from him. At times crooks ask you for directions; don't look away to point somewhere. Instead, tell him any information, without taking your eyes offs him. Thugs use all kinds of tricks to take you by surprise, always remember this.

In my opinion people become bullies in different ways, Personality occurrence and by accident. Some have personality disorders. The most dangerous bully in my view is the one I call the Opportunist bully, is the one you are most likely to encounter in the street. Just waiting for the opportunity to attack you verbally or physically.

Some bullies tactics includes:

1. Put down, insults, name calling
2. Hostile eye contact
3. Blame target of wrong doing

Disrespect target openly
You must keep in mind that most of the bullies are seen by their peers in the streets like in schools as "leaders"

These predators look to see if you are easy for assault, Rapist will pick a woman that does not walk with an assertive posture and appears to be very alert. Both are looking for easy prey.

The predator or bully hates to get disrespected, if he tries you and you tell him to get out of here you son of a b… or something to that matter he will take it like you have been disrespectful to his ego.

You are in real trouble now. Be assertive, don't confront him, look at him at the eyes, but do not try to "stare him down" Answer him verbally strongly, loudly and very assertively.

Like "I don't want any problems leave me alone! Or "Back off! and star moving away like the situation is over. This is the correct way to face a bully, or said something like this, I didn't mean it was a miss understanding, I'm on my way, Star moving away. Most of the time this could stop his pushing the situation especially if there are people in front as a witness.

Sometimes you have no other option but to protect yourself. I'm speaking here of parking lot circumstances, traffic dispute, somebody bumping into you, or someone cutting in front of you in a line. Not when your life or the life of someone in your family is at risk. In a situation of life and death, you have and must do whatever it takes to eliminate the situation.

Unfortunately, sometimes it takes more to defend yourself, but after talking to many of these troublemakers, it's a fact that most of them will go and look for an easier victim to pick on.

How the predator choose a victim:

The way you move, clothes, posture, low talking voice, if you are very polite, weak, and fragile, woman, and family man with wife and or children, these are signals to a predator that you are an easy target. If you don't follow this pattern the predator looks elsewhere. Rapists, muggers, abusers and bullies look for someone they can dominate and control.

Bullies Are Liars and Cowards!

There are three responses to a dangerous situation that only you must decide to take, there are:

Obedient -Getting out - Fighting

If you are aware of the situation around you, you will reduce by 97 % chance of being victimized someday. You don't have to live in fear, just make some adjustment,

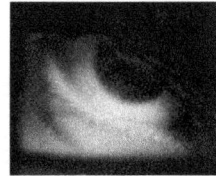

Make it part of your life, like breathing or blinking. You must do it automatically. Once you get used to do it you don't even have to think about it or even recall you did it, it will become part of you, but it may save your life or the ones you love.

Fear:

In a situation where you have to decide to fight or flight, your Adrenaline will make your heart rate higher, you will breathe faster and your blood pressure will rise. Your muscle will tense all over your body, you will sweat, and your mouth will dry up. Hands and legs most likely will tremble.

Your fear will be high; you won't be able to think clearly. That is why, fear and panic is what criminal intends to induce into you, making his attack easier.

The goal in self-defense is when nothing happens!

Sucker punch-The Most Dangerous Situation

No one can prepare for a surprise sucker punch. A sucker punch is an act of violence that you don't expect or you're unsuspecting of. This type of assault is its one of the most dangerous attacks a person can suffer.

The most dangerous opponent is the one that without giving any signals and no emotion walks close right up to you and punch you right in your face with no notice.

I watched on the late news on the 28th of July, at 7:01 PM a Surveillance video showing a man sucker punching a valet attendant at the Ocean Sky Resort at Fort Lauderdale hotel. The parking attendant said, "The men didn't want to pay to valet his truck". I really don't know what went on before the punch. I know that a punch like that can kill a man, especially by hitting his head on the pavement when he falls down.

Nowadays everybody knows about the gang-initiation thug of the Knockout punch. Where young violent gang members run up to their targets and deliver a surprise powerful knockout blow, while one of them film it. Then, post these videos on the internet.

Congested streets give these thugs the opportunity to strike, and cowardly run away. These delinquents will take advantage of noise, music, and activities to disguise the approaching attack, obstructing you from becoming aware. You should always try to walk in open areas, away from huge crowds. Try not to use phones or music gadgets, ear buds or headphones when walking on the streets, not blocking external noises.

Keep your eyes open, notice who is walking your way, how nearby, they are from you, remember, crooks target those inattentive, and those who appear as easy victims.

If you have an agitated dispute, and you see the verbal intensifies, there are a few things you must keep in mind to try to avoid a sucker punch, or at least make it less dangerous. Observe signals that will indicate your verbal fight is about to turn physical.

Check your antagonist's hands and arms. Are his arm up close to his waistline? Are his fists clenched? These are signals of an incoming punch. Standing within arm's reach will leave you in a weak position to a brutal sucker punch attack.

Step back a bit, he moves close to you, again, you move back a few steps, slowly back up and allow yourself distance between you and your foe. Also, when you move back do it at an angle, side way a bit, making it harder for him to punch you, at least with all his force.
 You must keep your hands up at your waistline, in a no disrespectful way, but ready to counter block, never in your pockets.

 A sucker punch it is hard to avoid, but you can try to make it less lethal.

Remember 2 steps:

1- Step back
2- In an angle if possible,
3- Hands up ready to protect your face and head.

"Distance is a powerful tactical tool"

Diffuse an aggressive situation suggestion

Keep in mind these tactics may not work all of the time. There are two types of expert's opinion; some experts don't consider any of these awareness ideas of response to be self-defense, they think that they don't work in real life as the assailant will become more aggressive realizing you are a weak person. The other group of experts thinks they work. I personally believe they work depending on the situation, place and time.

A-If you are facing an angry person, try to keep calm and control yourself, and instead control your words, in the hope that your provokers do the same.

B- Keep your distance, out of his punch reach, move back or sideways away from him, keep an adequate space so you can talk. Remember, if you are too close he may kick, punch or grab you. Distance is key here.

C-Apologize, try a solution. Sometimes is the best to use this approach to defuse an aggressive situation. Believe me, it is very hard to do, and most of the time it won't work.

D-Be ready. No matter how much you try, sometimes the crook does not want to hear you for a peaceful conclusion. You must be ready for a physical attack. If you can't walk away, you must defend yourself with all you can, remember yelling so people can see what is going on.

The supreme art of war is to subdue the enemy without fighting.

Sun Tzu

After the confrontation

The argument, confrontation or fight is over. You think, right? You must be very, very, careful here. You have to remain **alert** and in the fight long enough to make a safe withdrawal and make sure you are out of danger completely. This is something that most people do not do after an attack or confrontation, they think the attack is over when in reality is not or far away from being over. **Lookout**!

1-Don't turn your back on the attacker ever, when leaving the scene.

2-Find words to keep it calm, instead of insulting him

3-Never dare him or accept his bait to go out and fight

4-Find a way for him to leave with his pride up, important for bullies and thugs

5- Keep your guard up as you walk away from the confrontation site, even when getting into your car or when driving home

6-Call the police or emergency medical services if necessary and tell them the problem or situation as soon as possible

7-Keep your guard up and be into a lookout for a couple of days, to make sure the attacker is not planning revenge. Very important in the time we are living today

Remember, do not let your guard down not even for a second and don't trust your attacker whatsoever until you are save home. Keep your eyes open for a few days and you will not regret it.

Forgive your enemies, but never forget their names.
John F. Kennedy

Mental condition - Be ready

Be ready for anything. Violence can invade anyone's life at any time, and in any place. You must be attentive of your surroundings at all times. In every situation make mental notes of potential escape routes, items that can be used as weapons.

Prevention tips

Prevention tips are simple steps you must take to reduce the likelihood that you will become the victim of a crime.
I repeat myself; prevention and awareness are the two most powerful tactics in your arsenal against criminals.

Avoid dangerous people and dangerous places.

If you go to unsafe areas, particularly at night or visit locations where drugs and drunken men meet you are exposing yourself to high dangers.
For example, if you point your finger in someone's face in a street fight encounter, the bully is going to take it like you are trying to intimidate him.
Remember, for effective de-escalation, your entire body, mind, voice, choice of words, and emotions must be altogether.

You must convince a bully that you are willing to avoid the confrontation. Don't use words like "slow down" "stay cool," "shut up," "don't get any closer" Such worlds will likely make him very mad. Say please, "let's talk about this," or "I realize you are upset that was not my intension say "excuse me" when someone accidentally bumps into you on the street or in a bar. Or I'm sorry.

Eye contact- Look directly at the person's eyes. The eyes belonging, to criminal most of the time are chilling.

Don't overdo it.

I remember having looked into some people's eyes that were intensity fiery. Looking down or away suggest a lack of confidence. Continuous eye contact can be uncomfortable, but punctuated by occasional looking away will do the work

Body stance your posture tell others your message, stand straight, face the person. In a stand up for yourself leaning forward to present a stronger case than leaning away.

Gesticulation-A massage with appropriate gesture takes on added emphasis. Latin's and Italians use extroverted gesturing to describe a scene to emphasize specific points.

Voice sound-Volume-A whispered monotone will seldom convince another person you mean business.

Softness- Hesitation is a signal to others that you are unsure of yourself, control your voice.

Instant- Spontaneity is best. Try to confront the person as soon as you realize that you are going have to do it.

Issue- Say it and said it forcefully and very loud, the more people that heard it the better.

Be encourage- believe in yourself

Nothing will always work, but is much better to try than the alternative. Ask for help if you have to.

Your mind-set is your primary weapon
Jeff Cooper

The Criminal Silent Weapon

Brass Knuckles
A metal bar with fingers rings that fit over fingers allowing for a destructive blow. Very dangerous.

Billy Clubs
Hardwood pole similar to those carried by the police. Bones can be easily be shattered with a hit from the Billy Clubs.

Hat Pins
They are easily concealable and correctly use can cause death. Very hard to see and detect. Very dangerous.

Knife There are many styles, shapes and sizes. Experiences delinquent can use this weapon with amazing speed and skills Very dangerous, even for the person using it if it's not an expert with one.

Razors
A straight razor is a horrifying weapon. Very easy to conceal, hard to see and very dangerous to be stroked with one.

Razor blades
Single edge razor is easily hidden. It is difficult to see in the attacker's hand, but make no mistake it could be fatal. Very, very dangerous.

Saps
Sap is alike a sock full of sand. It delivers a very strong blow. If stroke on the face can knock you down with one strike or even kill you.

Umbrellas
An umbrella has a vast of concealed weapons, pistols, swords, and daggers.

These are some of the weapons improvised by the criminal mind.

The four principles of self defense

Awareness
Concentrate on your surroundings; what are you doing and what people around you are doing.

Avoidance
 Prevent an attack. For this you must use your brain to try to resolve the problem without a confrontation

Escape
To escape out of danger, stay as calm as you can and calculate your position and find ways of escaping.

Fight
Fight as a last result, when the three options above are not available or when you know your life or the life's of the one you love are in real danger.

Most people's response under attack is panic and chaos. The attacker, bully or predator knows this; they are counting on this to make the attack a success. Stay serene and use or do whatever it takes to get out.

If for some reason you are not able to stop the bully from getting a grab of you, the next thing he will try do is force you into the ground. You must stop him from doing this, if he succeeds your chances of getting out is almost none. So fight for your life.

The proper course of action, when under attack, is usually to Counterattack.
                                                                    Jeff Cooper

Self-defense for men

Self-defense for men, like self-defense for women and for children it is about the same. Develop and use skills that will prevent dangerous situations, most of the time.

If an assailant assaults you, and you can change from defensive to an aggressive strategy, physically and psychologically, you force the attacker to react to you and not you to him. He will be shocked, surprise, and taken by surprise. This could change the situation a little bit to your victory. Remember the crook wants a prey no an adversary.

If you are being mugged, or a family member next to you is attacked, and you are confronting risk of death, serious physical injury, or sexual assault you have the right to protect yourself or the other family member. If you fight back the crook, hit fast, powerfully, while moving to get away as rapidly as possible, yell every time you throw an attack, this will make you breath in and out, pumping oxygen to your body and muscle, and at the same time if you get hit in your gut, you won't go out of air, keep yelling "leave me alone", "let me go away," "Stop hitting me".

If you ever had to defend yourself or your family, you can't be too nice.

Your survival, or the survival of your loved ones, depends on your success, you must win. No matter the outcome you must win.

What this means is, if you have to fight you must hit, bite, punch over, over and over, hard brutally as you can. Self-defense is simple. There's no time to try to do complex movements! Period!

A man, is not worried about being attacked when he takes the dog for a walk, go to the market or return to his car in a parking lot, he doesn't worry most of the time. He is a men, he can defend himself. Who is going to attack him? Wrong! This is 99% of the men thinking.

The dilemma is that many men, of course, did not grow up in the circumstances where they would actually fight other young men.

Your safest choice is to try to use your awareness and intuition to avoid possible trouble. And it is important to know how to fight when you have no other choice.

For a man an insult, can be more than enough to get into a fight. The best self-defense for men in a situation like this, don't! Don't engage in such fights. Don't give an attacker an excuse.

If driving, please try not to give the crazy, incompetent driver the finger, do not tailgate him to show your impatience, or cut him off to retaliate against him for cutting you off, as you know you and me as done so many times. It's not worth it. How many times we heard this in the news, somebody pulling a gun out and killing the driver.

Leave your fighting for a death or life situation, a threat to your life, a sexual assault on you or a family member. When is a situation like that, you make your stand. You fight 100%. You must fight even with danger of death. Would you be willing to risk if your life or if your daughter or son was being dragged into a car by a predator or criminal? Of course you would! I know you wouldn't even think about it for a moment.

If what you are fighting over is not worth risking death, you must just walk away. Because in today's world the man you are fighting over an insult could be crazy and shoot you to death over an irrelevant offense.

Violence intensifies really fast, is erratic, in reality nobody wins. You probably will get hurt or even get killed, you may punch somebody, the guy fall, and he may hurt his head in the fall and died. Witnesses in front are going to declare that you hit first. As you can see this, it is a no a winning position.

Fighting should always be your last resort, when you have no other way out. Anything short of life or death situation should be passed, swallow your pride and walk away.

If you must fight, as soon as you can leave, leave and get yourself and the people important to you to safety at the first opportunity you have.

Distance

Keep at least five feet away from your attacker more if you can. Distance is a very important component in self -defense.

The ultimate triumph in self-defense is when nothing to happen! Or you defuse it, or escape. If you have to fight your way out of the situation makes it your last resort. However, give it all you have!

The male child is always coached to be strong, not to cry, to be brave. If one day the child comes in the house with a black eye, but he broke the neighborhood bully's nose, the father will feel very proud.

The athlete who participates in competitive sports knows that if he is aggressive and breaks the rule a little it is acceptable because what is important is to win. This is why some people grow up thinking is OK to be a bully.

Personal space/Close range defense

The assailant has a weapon like a knife, baseball bat or sharp object. He must get close to you, the quicker you move out of his range, the better. Place anything between you and your attacker; create as many obstacles as you can, chairs, tables, trash can, anything. Gaining time gives you chances to escape, to think how to solve the situation and to get help.

Control your distance

If the thug has a Baseball bat, for example, you have to control the space around you, by throwing things at him, moving away, yelling, be cautious running away; he may strike you in the back of your head. Be smart when you move away from him. Get away as fast and far away as soon as you can.

"An appeaser is one who feeds a crocodile hoping it will eat him last."
Sir Winston Churchill

Chapter2- Elevator/Stairs

Stairs are presumed to be fireproof and
probably they are also soundproof. I believe the
elevator is much safer than the stairs. Avoid
using stairs if you live in an apartment,
especially after hours.

In an elevator stand near the alarm buttons to be
able to get off at the next floor if something
happens. **DON'T** get on if you would be alone with someone that you
for some reason don't like or felt comfortable with. Wait until the
next one.

This is another place to be alert and on guard. When you get in situate
yourself closed to the door, no matter how you do it, get used to this,
if someone gets in that your instinct tells you don't like, get out, that's
your right, don't be shy, if the elevator stop in a floor you are not
going to, but someone gets in and for some motive again you don't
feel comfortable get out. You are only going to lose three or four
minutes of your time.

If you are standing close to the door and the controls
and somebody attacks you, block the controls with your
body, do whatever it takes to block the person from
stopping the elevator, be careful to press the alarm
button, it may stop the elevator trapping you with your
assailant. Never stand with your back to the other
passengers. Also, if you are ever attacked in an elevator
push all the buttons right away. This way you a have a better chance
to get away because it will be stopping at every floor and also because
someone will be able to see the situation you are in and may come to
your aide or call the police.

Some have also a phone, if it does, pick it up and just keep yelling
help, help, don't try to explain and lose precious moments explaining,
yelling, help will do. Also, you may use the phone as a weapon,
against the aggressor, resist, fight back, yell, he is not spec ting that,
he will be shocked and surprise, tear his shirt up, this will shake him
up and he would just want to escape, get out fast because the police

will be able to spot him fast with his shirt all in pieces, so he would be able to look for another victim more passive next time.
Again awareness is the trick here, keep your eyes open and never let your guard down. It's much better to get to your work or doctor appointment in four minutes late, than never make because you are in the hospital.

A friend of mine and I'm going to call him Nick, Nick was in Colombia about 10 years ago vacationing. He was drinking and partying in the hotel night club. After many drinks and dances he decided that t he had enough, he took the elevator , the elevator was empty, but by the time the door was going to close a man came running and holds it and got in.

What happens next as soon as the elevator begins to move, the man took a gun out, press the stop button, and rob him of all his money, jewelry and his wallet full of credit cards. It took the man, one or two minutes, then depress the stop button, and got out on the next floor, before he got out he pressed the elevator button and my friend went up.

Again, awareness could have been his best defense, as soon as the man got in, he should have gotten out, particularly in a foreign country, at that time of the night, what a coincidence of all of a sudden somebody wants to go up with you. He should have waited, got out and take another elevator with more people in it, use the stairs or waited, anyway he had spent hours in the club. What difference would make ten more minutes.

Dangerous!!!

Parking

Always park in well-lighted areas, and nearby to where you are going as possible. Be aware of your surroundings at all times.

Don't park between vans or trucks. This could be used by the predator as a hiring place from people's view.

Keep in mind that females and especially some today's teenagers can be delinquent too. Do not misestimate young men's and young woman. They can be dangerous, too.

Keep in mind the time when you are going to depart your work or the store. At the time you got in was very busy, but what about at 8:00pm or later? Always see the whole picture. Now is OK, but what about at 10:00pm?

Can somebody observe if you get robbed from the place you park? Can people passing by see you? Is there anything blocking the view of your car?

If possible walk out with a co-worker, a friend or just wait a couple of minutes to walk out with other peoples.

Give only the auto ignition key to parking attendants. Take out the house keys before giving the keys to the attendants; also do the same with the car mechanic.

If your car has a flat tire immediately leave, contact security personnel, the police or have a male friend escort you.

Be alert the whole time!

Cellular

If you have a cellular keep it in your hands. If you really scare make believe you are talking to someone. This probably will make the attacker think before launching his attack.

You could be talking with someone for real and get the police on his tail to soon.

Cellular is a big help against crime now a day if you know when to use it.

If you feel in danger at any time do not hesitate, dial the police, if something makes you feel uncomfortable, get into the car quickly, lock the doors, and drive away.

Prevent snatching

To prevent purse **snatching** you must carry a purse in a manner that makes it inaccessible, like wearing it under your coat. Women think that wearing a shoulder bag with the strap diagonally across their body is a good idea, but, is not, if someone grabs the purse and tries to run with it, the **strap** is going to catch around your **neck**. If you keep your purse close to your body and your arm over it makes it a little bit harder for someone to grab the purse.

Purse Cutting

I was eating at a famous restaurant in Miami, FL and the manager's wife came in crying because someone in the mall in a very prestigious store just had cut open her shoulder hanging purse with an X-Acto knife or surgical knife and remove her wallet with all her credit cards and some good amount of cash, by the time she realized it and called the police, these thieves had spent hundreds of dollars in her credit cards. The police looked over the store anti-thief camera tape, but these people were looking down or wearing hats or hair pieces the police said.

I heard the conversation, stood up and ask her if she remembers anything unusual, she said that she remember that at one time when

62

she was looking at some clothes in a table, a lady asks her opinion of a dresses, at the same time a man walked by her side making her move to the side, and told her he was sorry to inconvenience her, at the same time other men in front said a loud comment to the lady who just had asked the question.

All convened, at the same time working together to make her talk and give her visual distraction. It took them seconds.

What could she have done?

1- Not having her purse hanging almost in her back from her shoulder.

2- Being aware of the situation, three people all at the same time dealing with her? This should have been a red flag.

3- Last but very important right away hold her purse with her right hand and instantly move it over like swift it for a few minutes close to her chest or front of her body.

4- When the men ask her to move she should have moved away from the table so the men did not have to pass by her so closely.

Threats

Take any threats **seriously**. Report it to the police immediately. If you move to a new location, do not let your address or telephone number be known to anyone except the one real close and trusty to you, better to use a post office box for all of your correspondence.

"The error of one moment becomes the sorrow of a whole life"
Chinese Proverbs quote

The FBI's report: America's 15 most dangerous States.

Here are The Most Dangerous States in the United States According to the FBI's semiannual uniform crime report in 2016-2017.

The number of violent crimes increased by 5.3% during the first six months of 2016

15. Florida

No.15spot. Florida has some of the highest reported crime, with 2,758 violent crimes, 52 murders, 703 robberies, 1,752 aggravated assault cases, and 15,340 property crimes in 2016, according to FBI crime statistics.

14. Mississippi

No.14spot. Jackson, Mississippi, has some of the highest reported crime, with 677 violent crimes, 27 murders, 42 robberies, 297 aggravated assault cases, and 311 property crimes in 2016, according to FBI crime statistics.

13. Oklahoma

No.13spot. According to FBI crime statistics in 2016, among cities with 100,000 people or more, Oklahoma City has some of the highest reported crime, with 2,462 violent crimes, 30 murders, 547 robberies, 1,658 aggravated assault cases, and 12,436 property crimes in 2016.

12. Oregon

No.12spot. Among cities with 100,000 people or more, Eugene, Oregon, has some of the highest reported crime in the state, with 285 violent crimes, two murders, 58 robberies, 183 aggravated assault cases, and 2,941 property crimes in 2016, according to FBI crime statistics.

11. Louisiana

No.11spot Among cities with 100,000 people or more, New Orleans has some of the highest reported crime in Louisiana, with 2,041 violent crimes, 67 murders, 685 robberies, 990 aggravated assault cases, and 7,586 property crimes in 2016, according to the FBI.

10. South Dakota

No.10 spot Sioux Falls has some of the highest reported crime in South Dakota, with 460 violent crimes, two murders, 57 robberies, 331 aggravated assault cases, and 2,664 property crimes in 2016, according to FBI crime statistics.

9. Delaware

No.9 spot Delaware is #9 according to FBI crime statistics in 2016. Delaware, one of the state's cities that have received a lot of negative attention when it comes to crime is Wilmington, Delaware. In fact, a few years back, it was called "Murder Town USA" by Newsweek.

8. Missouri

No. 8 spot is Missouri. Among cities with 100,000 people or more, Kansas City, Missouri, has some of the highest crime in the state, with 3,668 violent crimes, 51 murders, 862 robberies, 2,577 aggravated assault cases in 2016. And it had 9,204 property crimes in 2016, according to FBI crime statistics.

7. Nevada

No. 7 spot is Nevada. FBI crime statistics revealed among cities with 100,000 people or more, the Las Vegas metro area has some of the highest reported crime, with 7,277 violent crimes, 83 murders, 2,537 robberies, 3,922 aggravated assault cases, and 22,234 property crimes in 2016.

6. Tennessee

No. 6 spot is Tennessee. FBI crime statistics revealed among cities with 100,000 people or more, Memphis, Tennessee, has some of the highest reported crime, with 5,733 violent crimes, 88 murders, 1,537 robberies, 3,879 aggravated assault cases, and 16,833 property crimes in 2016.

5. Michigan

No. 5 spot is Michigan. FBI crime statistics revealed among cities with 100,000 people or more, Detroit has some of the highest reported crime, with 5,409 violent crimes, 103 murders, 1,130 robberies, 3,909 aggravated assault cases, and 13,442 property crimes in 2016.

4. New Mexico

No. 4 spot is New Mexico. FBI crime statistics revealed among cities with 100,000 people or more, Albuquerque, New Mexico, has some of the highest reported crime, with 2,897 violent crimes, 32 murders, 847 robberies, 1,825 aggravated assault cases, and 17,888 property crimes in 2016.

3. Arkansas

No. 3 spot is Arkansas. FBI crime statistics revealed among cities with 100,000 people or more, Little Rock, Arkansas, has some of the highest reported crime, with 1,415 violent crimes, 16 murders, 302 robberies, 1,018 aggravated assault cases, and 6,476 property crimes in 2016.

2. South Carolina

No. 2 spot is South Carolina. FBI crime statistics revealed among cities with 100,000 people or more, North Charleston, South Carolina, has some of the highest reported crime, with 435 violent crimes, 15 murders, 136 robberies, 244 aggravated assault cases, and 2,961 property crimes in 2016.

1. Alaska

No. 1 spot, Alaska wins the as the most dangerous state. FBI crime statistics revealed among cities with 100,000 people or more, Anchorage, Alaska, has some of the highest reported crime, with 1,692 violent crimes, nine murders, 326 robberies, 6,853 property crimes, and 1,055 aggravated assault cases in 2016.

The FBI's 10 Most Dangerous Cities in 2017

This is data from the FBI in 2017. Data only considers cities with a population of over 100,000. States with cities with a population of less than 100,000 are excluded.

The FBI's 10 Most Dangerous Cities in 2017

Top 10 Most Dangerous U.S. Cities, by Violent Crimes:

1. St. Louis, Missouri

2. Memphis, Tennessee

3. Rockford, Illinois

4. Baltimore, Maryland

5. Detroit, Michigan

6. Kansas City, Missouri

7. Milwaukee, Wisconsin

8. Little Rock, Arkansas

9. Stockton, California

10. Oakland, California

13 Of The Nation's 100 Most Dangerous Cities are In Florida.

Florida, where I live, contains more of the nation 100 most dangerous cities — a total of 13. Cited by #

25 Opa locka, FL
24 Homestead, FL
28 Daytona Beach, FL
40 Riviera Beach, FL
47 Lake Worth, FL
54 Fort Myers, FL
58 Fort Pierce, FL
63 Miami, FL
72 Miami Beach, FL.The most dangerous city in Florida.
82 Tallahassee, FL
86 North Miami, FL
95 Panama City, FL
97 Orlando, FL

Intimidating neighborhoods in Miami, FL, I have not only driven through them, but also walked the streets.

Overtown   Goulds-South of Perrine.
Carol City   Little Hattie.
Opa-Locka   Little Havana,
West Grove   Liberty City.
Hialeah.   West Little River.

USA Cities

Some dangerous cities and neighborhoods I have visited.

California

Los Angeles   Downtown
South   Little Tokyo,
East la   Central LA
Vernon/Main

New Orleans

I walked the French Quarter multiple times in the evening or late at night, just walked around looking at the surrounding of the French Quarter.

Some of the places I venture into, Downtown, East, Mid-City, 9th Ward, Bywater, St. Bernard (7th Ward), Lafitte (6th Ward), Iberville (4th Ward)

Downtown
Central City
Carrolton

City: Atlanta, Georgia

Numerous people are shocked to find that Atlanta is one of the highest dangerous cities in the United States, placing 6th in the top ten lists for cities with the highest rate of violent crime.

Memphis, Tennessee

Memphis has one of the highest violent crime rates in the country: 1,583 per 100,000 residents. Memphis continues to be one of the most dangerous cities to visit.

Recent FBI crimes reports

FBI Crime Report 2016, across the USA

A violent crime was committed every 26.3 seconds.

A murder every 33.5 minutes

A rape every 4.2 minutes,

A robbery every 1.6 minutes

An aggravated assault every 41. 3 seconds.

Every year 1 in 5 families is a victim of **Crime**.

4.5 million Dog Attacks yearly

Crimes happen typically between 9 P.M. and 3 a.m.

A **woman** who **fights back** gains an 86% chance of avoiding the **rape** and incurs a little chance of additional injury.

Most injuries occur before the woman starts fighting back.

 Women using knives or guns in self-defense were raped less than 1% of the time.

 Persons age 16 -19 are raped at 35 times that of persons age 50 64.

Weapon:

In about 1: 4 (26%) of violent crimes, a weapon was present.

The Most Dangerous Neighborhoods in the United States

That's according to Neighborhoodscout.com, which just released a
list in 2015 based on the number of local violent crimes reported to
the FBI data from all 17,000 local law enforcement agencies, and the
population of each city.

You must keep in mind that even the cities with the highest crime
rates can have relatively safe neighborhoods.

New York, N.Y.

Most tourists visiting New York City simply cannot avoid Midtown.
This is the heart of the City, Unfortunately; it is also a prime spot for
pick-pocketing.
Vinegar Hill (Brooklyn)
Downtown Brooklyn (Brooklyn)
Greenwood Heights (Brooklyn)
East New York (Brooklyn)
Ocean Hill (Brooklyn)
Brownsville (Brooklyn)
Navy Hill (Brooklyn)
Brooklyn Heights (Brooklyn)
Theatre District / Times Square (Manhattan)
Koreatown (Manhattan)
Garment District (Manhattan)
Union Square (Manhattan
Midtown Manhattan
Greenwich Village (Manhattan)
Harlem (Upper Manhattan)
Washington Heights (Manhattan)
Flatiron District (Manhattan)

Longwood (Bronx)
Hunts Point (Bronx)

Chicago, Ill.
Chicago, Ill.
Neighborhood: 66th St./Yale Ave.
Neighborhood: State St./Garfield Blvd
Springfield, Ill.
Neighborhood: Cook St./11th St.

Philadelphia, Pa.
Neighborhood: Broad St./Dauphin St.

Memphis, Tenn.
Neighborhood: Bellevue Blvd. /Lamar Ave.
Neighborhood: Warford St. /Mount Olive Rd.

Virginia
We took data from the annual FBI report.
The data shows that these six places are currently the most dangerous in Virginia:

Richmond, Va.
Neighborhood: Church Hill
Norfolk
Roanoke
Richmond
Franklin

New Jersey
The most dangerous places are,
City of Asbury Park
City of Newark
City of Bridgeton.
City of Woodbury

Nevada
Las Vegas

The Most Dangerous Neighborhoods-International

Dominican Republic
Santo Domingo
San Pedro de Macorís
Puerto Plata
La Romana
Boca Chica

Mexico

Mexico City
Mexico is the fifth most dangerous country in Latin America.
Dangerous as in any big city, Mexico subways, looks very unsafe to
me after dark.

Tepito- Few outsiders dare venture after dark.
Condesa
Roma

Colonia Centro -- the heart of Mexico City, includes the areas in and
around the Alameda Park and the zócalo, the capital's historic central
square.

San Angel	Cuernavaca	Xochimilco
Chapultepec Park	Acapulco	Cozumel
Polanco	Taxco	Mérida.

Acapulco, Mexico
Acapulco is scenic. Nonetheless, it is known as the drug-related
murder capital of Mexico. Reports claim, there are about 300 paid
killers in the Acapulco region.

Cuba
Sometimes there are pickpockets and scams. There are no-go places
in Cuba as well. People should be careful not to be lulled into a false
sense of security – be as cautious in Cuba as you would anywhere.

Habana City	Vedado	Habana del Este
La Habana Vieja	Plaza de la	& Playas del
Paseo del Prado	Revolución	Este
Parque Central	Miramar	
Centro Habana		

The area around the Morro Castle.
Habana del Este, Alamar, Cojímar.
Regla
Casablanca.
Marianao
Varadero
Pinar Del Rio

Streetlights are virtually nonexistent; avoid the dark alleys and side streets of Habana after dark. Recently, there have been reports of muggings and pick-pocketing in Havana; be aware of your surroundings.

Unaccompanied female should not walk alone through Centro Habana late at night, unless you're walking through the tourist section. Still, given the vast economic gap between Cubans and tourists, you should be careful about where you walk and whom you engage.

It is best not to wear much jewelry or make other showy signs of wealth.

Bolivia

La Paz is one of the highest cities in the world.

El Alto, Av. Buenos Aires, El Alto has narrow streets and poor houses, built of mud and bricks.

Copacabana
Indians, indigenous, people who speak Quechua or Aymara.

Lake Titicaca on a traditional Torta Reed boat.

Road closures and protests

The days I spend in 1971 in Bolivia some of the roads were obstructed by a strike by the campesinos (peasant farmers) I had to ride many times in an open truck full of indigenous people or native Bolivians.

I stood out like crazy; I was the only non-Indian men in the truck. I also navigated the Lake Titicaca in a Torta Reed boat with an indigenous man from Bolivia to Peru, many years before becoming kind of a Tourist Place. It was lonely and intimidating back then.

Titicaca is a large, deep lake in the Andes. It is situated at a very high altitude, at over 3800 meters above sea level. It is often called the highest navigable lake in the world. The lake is located at the northern end of the Altiplano basin high in the Andes on the border of Peru and Bolivia.

I also stayed in a little town high in the mountain with no electricity or water. Walking outside at 9:00 PM was dark, isolated, like a ghost town. You could only hear dogs howling in the distance.

I also drove through the most dangerous road in the world, Bolivia to the Amazon. I felt I was in another Planet!

Peru

Civil Unrest
Keep your eyes open for spontaneous protests that occur frequently in Lima and other cities in the interior of Peru.

Transportation strikes can occur at a moment's notice. American citizens are advised to avoid large crowds and demonstrations and are strongly encouraged to maintain a high level of vigilance.

Most dangerous districts:
Rímac, San Juan de Miraflores.

As you can see from the list above, I have visited many Countries including questionable neighborhoods where I use my technique awareness system to stay out of trouble.

Guatemala City

The capital of Guatemala, this city has several of the best museums, several governments have released travel advisories cautioning against visiting because of the crime. Theft, armed robbery, and carjacking are common. Fake taxis are operated by criminals with the intent on robbing, or even raping their passengers.

Santiago de Cali, Colombia

Better known as Cali, due to mafia rivalries, violence in this city is common, with riots caused by militarized drug cartels and insurgents.

Kingston Jamaica

A city with a vibrant culture and great music, still crime is a problem in the city. Robbery, assault, gang violence, and drug trafficking are all issues there.

Nelson Mandela Bay, South Africa

Ranked second in South Africa's most violent cities, tourists should be careful at the beachfront zone, theft, mugging is a constant problem.

San Pedro Sula, Honduras

This city is recognized for illegal drug and gangs. Tourists should be vigilant while visiting the city. Homicidal violence in Honduras had an average of 20 homicides per day in 2012.

Maturin, Venezuela

Maturin has a crisis with drug trafficking, Petty crime and theft also are very frequent on the streets at night.

Valencia, Venezuela

Murder, homicide, and kidnapping are everyday occurrences.

Caracas, Venezuela

Venezuela capital city. It is an interesting place, gang conflicts have placed the city in disaster, The United Nations claim, and it is the South American country with the above average number of homicides.

Kabul, Afghanistan

Kabul city is explosive and unreliable. Terrorism and bomb assaults on hotels and embassies are common.

Durban, South Africa

Crimes there include thefts, ATM scams, home invasion, and murder. Hijacking and armed robberies are also reported regularly.

San Salvador

Crimes include mugging, extortion; car theft, home invasion, and highway assault are frequently. Warnings traveling advice to San Salvador have been released by some governments.

Porto Alegre, Brazil

Porto Alegre is one of the most populated cities in Brazil, is also with the highest rate of homicides than all other larger Brazilian cities; crime information in the city are not exactly for the reason that most residents do not inform crimes to the authorities.

Karachi, Pakistan

Karachi is the capital and the largest financial city of Pakistan. Kidnapping, murder, extortion, and illegal drugs are all there. Armed muggings are frequent in the city.

Cape Town, South Africa

Rape, assault, murder, pickpocketing and mugging are frequently there.

FAKE TAXIS

In Cities like Mexico, Quito, Peru, keep your eyes open.

According to Forbes List

According to the latest information, six in 10 women in major Latin American city data, they've been physically harassed while using transportation systems, with Bogota, Colombia, found to have the highest unsafe public transportation, followed by Mexico City and Lima, Peru.

Aggressive Offense: Violent crime, like carjacking, assault, sexual assault, and armed robbery is common in Lima and other large cities

Keep this in mind when traveling.

The USA Embassy is conscious of testimonies of women being sexually assaulted where they were staying, or once their beverages were drugged while visiting taverns or discotheque. Women travelling solo must avoid environments where they are helpless due to weakened judgment or isolation.

Struggle to fight muggings often incites more violence. "Express kidnappings," this is when crooks kidnaps victims and seek to obtain money from their bank accounts by the use of automatic teller machines, this occurs frequently.

There have occurred significance occasions of armed assault, rape, other sexual assault, of U.S. citizens and other foreign tourists. Again, keep vigilant and very watchful.

Ecuador

High Crime Rate
Quito possesses an extremely high crime rate, even when considered to mostly big South American cities. The usually common crime against tourists is pickpocketing, by speedy hands or intimidation. Ecuador is considered "critical" for the crime by the State Department. Crimes against U.S. civilians, in the past year have varied from petty theft to violent offenses, involving armed theft, house invasion, sexual assault, and numerous cases of murder and attempted assassination.

Ask for directions to only families or women with children.

Traveling Smart

1- Write your work address in luggage tags instead of your home address.

2-Ask flight attendants on the plane about the safety of your destination before you actually arrive.

3-Always place your belongings on your car seat right away then get in the car

4- Make sure you arrive at your destination before getting out of a taxi. Pay while still in the car; make sure you've gotten the proper change.

5-Stay close and keeps an eye to your belonging when passing through airport security. Never take your eyes from them.

6- Sitting in a restaurant or other public area, place your carry-on bag on the floor and place your foot through the strap; don't leave it loose. Same in the restroom. Very important, especially in a public restroom.

7- Bring your own mobile phone or rent one. Place the police # on speed dial. Very important.

8- If renting a car, park so you won't have to back out. It makes for a speedier escape.

GENERAL ADVICE

1-Must people only just check the weather of their destination; also learn when the **sun rises** and **sets**. This is a **must** if you are in an unfamiliar place.

2-Check onto the Internet and obtain **safety info** about a place you're planning to visit.

> ***Self-defense is not only our right; it is our duty.***
> ***Ronald Reagan***

Definition 2015

In the FBI's Uniform Crime Reporting (UCR) Program, violent crime is composed of four offenses: murder and no negligent manslaughter, rape, robbery, and aggravated assault. The data presented in *Crime in the United States* reflect violent crimes are murder and no negligent manslaughter, rape, robbery, and aggravated assault, followed by the property crimes of burglary, larceny-theft, and motor vehicle theft.

The FBI's 2015 Uniform Crime Report that 1,197,704 violent crimes were committed in 2015, up 3.9% from 2014. Violent crime rates are by no means uniform across the country. Some of the nation's cities are far more dangerous than others.

For every 100,000 U.S. residents, 372 of these crimes were committed in 2015.

The UCR Program counts one offense for each victim of a rape, attempted rape, or assault with intent to rape, regardless of the victim's age.

Overview

In 2015, an estimated 1,197,704 violent crimes occurred nationwide, an increase of 3.9 percent from the 2014 estimate.

There were an estimated 372.6 violent crimes per 100,000 inhabitants in 2015, a rate that rose 3.1 percent when compared with the 2014 estimated violent crime rate.

Aggravated assaults accounted for 63.8 percent of violent crimes reported to law enforcement in 2015. Robbery offenses accounted for 27.3 percent of violent crime offenses; rape accounted for 7.5 percent; and murder accounted for 1.3 percent.

Firearms were used in 71.5 percent of the nation's murders, 40.8 percent of robberies, and 24.2 percent of aggravated assaults.

Robbery

The FBI's Uniform Crime Reporting (UCR) Program defines robbery as the taking or attempting to take anything of value from the care, custody, or control of a person or persons by force or threat of force or violence and/or by putting the victim in fear.

Rape

All rape data submitted in 2015

There were an estimated 90,185 rapes (legacy definition) reported to law enforcement in 2015. This estimate was 6.3 percent higher than the 2014 estimate.

Property Crime

In 2015, there were an estimated 7,993,631 property crime offenses in the nation. The 2-year trend showed that property crime offenses declined 2.6 percent in 2015 when compared with the 2014 estimate.

In 2015, the rate of property crime was estimated at 2,487.0 per 100,000 inhabitants, a 3.4 percent decrease when compared with the 2014 estimated rate.

Larceny-theft accounted for 71.4 percent of all property crimes in 2015. Burglary accounted for 19.8 percent, and motor vehicle theft for 8.9 percent.

Property crimes in 2015 resulted in losses estimated at $14.3 billion.

Motor Vehicle Theft

Examples include sport utility vehicles, automobiles, trucks, buses, motorcycles, motor scooters, all-terrain vehicles, and snowmobiles. Motor vehicle theft does not include farm equipment, bulldozers, airplanes, construction equipment, or water craft such as motorboats, sailboats, houseboats, or jet skis. The taking of a motor vehicle for temporary use by people having lawful access excluded from this definition.

Overview

There were an estimated 707,758 thefts of motor vehicles nationwide in 2015. The estimated rate of motor vehicle thefts was 220.2 per 100,000 inhabitants.

The estimated number of motor vehicle thefts increased 3.1 percent in 2015 when compared with the 2014 estimates.

More than $4.9 billion was lost nationwide to motor vehicle thefts in 2015. The average dollar loss per stolen vehicle was $7,001.

In 2015, of all motor vehicles stolen, 74.7 % were automobiles.

The 2015 statistics show the estimated rate of violent crime was 372.6 offenses per 100,000 inhabitants, and the property crime rate was 2,487.0 offenses per 100,000 inhabitants. The violent crime rate rose 3.1 percent compared with the 2014 rate, and the property crime rate declined 3.4 percent.

Submitted data in 2015

A high-level summary of the statistics submitted, as well as estimates for those agencies that did not report, follows:

In 2015, there were an estimated 1,197,704 violent crimes. Murder and non-negligent manslaughter increased 10.8 percent when compared with estimates from 2014.

Rape and aggravated assault increased 6.3 percent and 4.6 percent, respectively, while robbery increased 1.4 percent.

Nationwide, there were an estimated 7,993,631 property crimes.

Burglaries dropped 7.8 percent, and larceny-thefts declined 1.8 percent, but motor vehicle thefts rose 3.1 percent.

Collectively, victims of property crimes (excluding arson) suffered losses estimated at $14.3 billion in 2015.

The FBI estimated that law enforcement agencies nationwide made 10.8 million arrests, excluding traffic violations, in 2015.

The arrest rate for violent crime was 157.2 per 100,000 inhabitants, and the arrest rate for property crime was 458.9 per 100,000 inhabitants.

By violent criminal offense, the arrest rate for murder and non-negligent manslaughter was 3.5 per 100,000 inhabitants; rape 7.1; robbery, 29.7; and aggravated assault, 117.0 per 100,000 inhabitants.

By property crime offense, the arrest rate for burglary was 67.5 per 100,000 inhabitants; larceny-theft, 364.5; and motor vehicle theft, 24.2. The arrest rate for arson was 2.8 per 100,000 inhabitants.

In 2015, there were 13,160 law enforcement agencies that reported their staffing levels to the FBI. These agencies reported that, as of October 31, 2015, they collectively employed 635,781 sworn officers and 277,380 civilians, a rate of 3.3 employees per 1,000 inhabitants.

Among some of the other statistics contained in *Crime in the United States, 2015*:

- The estimated number of murders in the nation was 15,696, 1.3%

- During the year, there were an estimated 90,185 rapes, 7.5%

- There was an estimated 327,374 robbery nationwide, which accounted for an estimated $390 million in losses.

- Firearms were used in 71.5 percent of the nation's murders, 40.8 percent of robberies, and 24.2 percent of aggravated assaults.

- Property crimes resulted in losses estimated at $14.3 billion. The total value of reported stolen property (i.e., currency, jewelry, motor vehicles, electronics, (firearms) was $12,420,364,454.

- Electronics, firearms) was $12,420,364,454.

How I kept safe in these cities

The strategic goal was that **I have always been on my guard.**

I have always flag down a reputable taxi.
I kept my money in my jean's front pocket.
I never use a backpack; I did not want to identify myself as a tourist!!
I did not look at a map or visitors' guide in the street. If you are lost walk into a store, restaurant, or bathroom. Be careful, who is watching you.
I was careful when using an ATM's machine. When using ATMs always be aware of people around you, what are they staring?
I tried to look and appear confident, try to look confident, even if you don't feel it.
I crossed the street right away and walked the other way for a couple of minutes if I thought someone was following me.
I was careful every time I used the restroom, and made sure no one follow me there.
I tried to always use the restroom in a reputable hotel or restaurant.
I never visited a bar or lounge by myself.
I kept my camera in my pants pocket at all times.
I Ignored side roads after dark, stick to wider boulevards with street lighting.
I was always careful, especially at night, and who walked into the elevator with me.
I made sure not to step into the elevator with strange looking people. I tried to wait for a family, or at least a couple.

Fear is the father of courage and the mother of safety.
Henry H Tweedy

Pickpockets

You really have to take precaution for this. If all of a sudden you are surrounded by a small group, move your hands right away to cover your pocket, phone, or handbag. Stop, move right away from this group, and try to stand against a store window.

This is what they do, they encircle you, one smack against your shoulder, when passing you, and so you don't feel the one behind you or next to you go in your purse, reaching for your phone or camera.

Most of the time this happens in Museums, Subways, sidewalk by a mayor chain store, tourist attraction or park, but can happen anywhere. **Be Extra Careful** at the Bus Terminals.

Avoiding Pickpockets:

1-Use a belt pocket-or uses the pant front pocket, never use your back pocket.

2- Don't presume because somebody is nicely dress you can trust them.

3-Never hang over your purse from your shoulder; never dangle your purse, backpack over the back of your chair.

4- Stay away from crowds where people can brush up against you and pickpocket you.

5- Under no circumstances count your money in public. If you need to count your money or check your wallet, do it inside a stall in the bathroom, or even better in your hotel room.

6-keep the money you're intending to spend set apart from the rest of your money.

7- Make certain to close the zipper in your purse when in public.

8-Be cautious all the time, pickpockets frequently use kids to distract you and another to rob you.

9- Always walk facing the traffic. Using this tactic, no cars can sneak up behind you to commit a crime. You prevent thieves on scooters snatching your handbags as they drive past you.

Tips for Women/ Men Travelers

HOTEL

Hotels near high-profile locations are considered to favor terrorist targets.

 Keep some food or chips and water in your hotel room as soon as you can, just in case something happens and you can't get out for a while.
 It is a good idea to keep the number 911 for the United States, In Canada, 911 do not work like in other countries. The EU has formally implemented 112 for emergencies, if you are in Europe, keep that number handy.

How to Be Safe in a Foreign Country

Be vigilant at night if you are a woman, this is the most unsafe time in every country. If you are not familiar with the area or don't know the neighborhood, don't go, most of the crimes activities take place late at night. Avoid late-night pubs, and make sure to take precautions against date rape.

Sexual encounters precautions for men and woman, sexually transmitted diseases are common across the world, in particular among prostitutes. The only guaranteed protection is not having sex, if you do, wear or require your partner to use protection.

Avoid having drinks, doing drugs that make you disoriented in any way. You will be more vulnerable because you're not completely alert.

1-Stay in a hotel in a well-trafficked street neighborhood, restaurants and late-night stores mean -traffic, people, company, if your hotel location is by business offices, this is a bad idea because it means darkness and loneliness at night. Beware!

2- If you're not sure about the zone of your hotel, do not ask the person in reservations. Call a close by restaurant, and ask whether a woman can walk around at night.

3-No one should be able to overhear a name, room number, or other personal information when you register at the front desk.

4-For protection and privacy your room number should be written on the key envelope, not mentioned aloud for everybody around to hear. Very Important.

5-When you are making your reservation, make sure or find out if the parking lot is well lit and secure.

Find out if there's valet parking, if they have one, use it, even if it costs a little bit more.

6-If you are one of those folks who like to visit the hotel gym, be careful, is not a good idea to be alone in the gym. Never go alone. If you must go, go when the gym is the most full of activity. Don't be the last one to leave.

7-Travel light –Much better than taking a big heavy suitcase

8- **Keep your personal information secret.** Don't tell anyone you are traveling alone. Don't tell anyone where you are staying, where you are planning to go and when you are going. No matter how honest an individual appears.

9-Try to blend with the local, don't look like a tourist. Study and dress how the locals dress. You don't want to draw attention to yourself.

10- Keep your eyes open-Be extreme caution.

11- Select hotels/motel with doors that open to the interior hall instead to a parking lot. Make copies of your documentation, passport, travel itinerary, tickets, credit cards, driver's license, and this will help you recover any documents stolen, keep copies in separate locations, and safe.

12- According to the experts second floor rooms are safer than those on the first floor. I'm not too sure, if you get to your room late at night the less time you spent in the hall the better. That is why sometimes I don't agree on this one with the experts. Personally, when possible I always request first floor room.

13-Check your room every time you go back to it.

14-Always secure your door from the inside. Protect your room; place a chair against the doorknob. Leave a "do not disturb" sign on your door when you leave so that people think you're in there. Set the TV on at a low volume, so individuals cannot tell if your room is occupied or not.

15- When you enter your room check if anything at all looks suspicious or unsafe, leave right away to the front desk, ask for an escort, a security or call the police if you have to.

16-Avoid traveling with jewelry that a robber could use to identify you as a potential target. Don't wear unnecessary or pricey jewelry.

17- Prevent at all cost revealing your travel intentions so a vigilant predator can't be listening to your conversation.

18-Smart phone- Good idea is to buy a phone case charger that help your phone last as long as possible. Outfitting your phone with one is a good idea especially when traveling.

Ability is nothing without opportunity.
Napoleon Bonaparte

Woman Traveling

Visit locations and first-class hotels with excellent reviews. Share with a family member or friend your travel plan.

If you're arriving late at night, try to have a transfer car from the hotel to pick you up. Be extra cautious when requesting room service.

If you're renting a car, refill your gas tank, never allowed it to be less than half full tank.

If you are grabbing a taxi, make a simulated call and say something like, almost there, now I'm in a yellow, or white taxi (describe the company and color) crossing by boulevard X or by naming the store, I'll be there in xxxx, time. So the car driver believes you are meeting someone at your destination, and knows your whereabouts.

Traveling Tips

Violent crimes against women/men happen in the best and worst hotels around the world. Predators may play the part of a hotel member of staff, push the way in through an open or unlocked door, or obtain a pass key to the room.

As with home safety, never open your door unless you are certain the person on the other side is legitimate, and always try to carry a door wedge with you when you travel. A wedge is stronger than the door it secures.

Plan your trip in advance so you don't have to be standing around in public spaces, exposed to crime and thieves for prolonged time.

How to Be Safe in a Foreign Country

Travel abroad-it is a good idea to inform your Embassy or Consulate of your trip details, so in an emergency they can keep you informed if any civil unrest situations occur. Get the addresses and phone numbers of your country's embassy and military bases before your arrival to a foreign country.

Mark the spot of your embassy on the map and the directions of how to get there. Learn the location of the Embassy, ATM, hospital locations, and other ways to get to your hotel.

Travel Security Tips:

A- Travel during specific hours to avoid reaching your destination at night.

B- Select your rented car close to the airport terminal, or better yet at the airport.

C- Always stay in quality hotels. Never accept a room in a remote section of the hotel. Brace the door with a chair when going to bed.

D-Do not answer the door except, you know who is knocking and you can trust that person.

E- If you use a handbag, tuck it under your arm. Keep money in your front pockets.
If someone does grab your purse, let it go.

F- Dress in an informal way when possible. Avoid wearing ethnic or religious clothing.

G-Smartphone- there are a number of devices that increase your phone durability and help your phone last as long as possible. Outfitting your phone with one is a good idea, especially when traveling.

H- Documents Carry. Don't keep your credit cards, cash, and passport all in the same spot. Never flash cash anywhere.

I- Keep your wallet in the front pants pocket, not in the back pocket.

Cash

Cash many times is the only way outside the country to pay for taxis, local bus fares, foods or marketplaces. Take easy money to exchange, like $10.00 or $20.00 bills. You will find adequately places overseas to exchange money, like hotels, airports.

Take only a few credit cards, and only the one you are intending to use. Make a note of the emergency # in the back of the card in case they get stolen and you can't find it, or you forget to write it down, just call the bank and ask for it, there is a free international number you can call.

Keep in mind that taking cash is not as secure as traveling checks or US credit cards. Travelers checks sometimes turn out to be a hassle because a lot of merchants don't want to bother with the process. Never let your card out of your sight to prevent being a victim of a rip-off. This includes a waitress or a store clerk. If you notified the card company fast of a stolen card you will not be responsible for any purchase the thieves may have purchased. American card almost works everywhere in the world.

You have the same protection if you use a credit card abroad as when you use it in the USA.

Attempt to buy civil unrest, travel insurance; most travel insurance has a detailed exclusion for civil unrest. There are some policies that you are able to obtaining that will cover this event. It is worth the additional money if you are traveling to a problematic place.

Keep your eyes open at all times. Remember, you are a visitor, the predator probably knows that city like the palms of his hands. Be careful what you tell strangers. Don't tell any stranger the hotel you are staying in. Don't meet them there, meet them somewhere else, and never go alone.

Be careful what you drink, make sure to never take your eyes away from your drink. If you leave for the bathroom, when you come back, order another drink. Don't ever drink the one you left on the table before you excuse yourself. Don't trust anyone; don't believe anything a stranger tells you.

If you are going to take a taxi, take it during the hours of the day. At night, try to avoid it if possible, visit places within a walking distance from your hotel at night, if it is in a good neighborhood walk early. Don't come back too late. Leave the far away trips for the daytime hours. Don' stay at the bar or night club too late. Don't drink too much. Always think ahead of the game.

Lonely-dark-danger

When you get to your room, check it over before taking a shower or going to sleep. When you meet new friends always make sure you are close by someone you really trust. No matter the appearances or the way thing seems to seem. Be careful!

No matter where you are, your personal and family security should be a top priority. You don't have to walk around paranoid; just by being alert will help you avoid trouble. Avoid traveling with jewelry, or any valuable that a predator could use to identify you as a potential target. Common sense and awareness are the best protection against terrorism while traveling.

Trust, but verify
Ronald Reagan

Planes-Ships-Trains

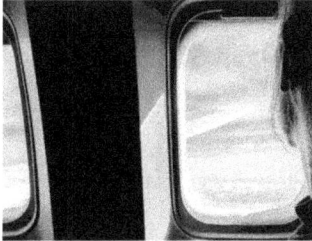

Airplanes-Select a seat near the center of the plane, investigations has shown the midsection is the most survival locations .Check visually where the exits are.

Ships- Choose a cabin above the water line, this is the safest option. Learn where the emergency escape routes are. Pinpoint life preservers and the life rafts location.

Trains-incidents confirmed that the center of the train is the best survival section to be. Learn the escape windows and exit doors.

Keep your eyes open!!

Traveling Tips

Maintaining awareness

Many people, who keep good awareness security at home, mentally let their guards down when they travel. Since they are relaxing and enjoying. Don't let this occurs to you.

Do not exchange your money with unlawful operators.

Buy bottled water. Water could make you ill, especially for children and seniors. If you buy water from a vendor in the streets, make sure that the cap is still attached to the bottle, many times they fool you.

Understand corrects Laws

When doing your destination research, review, correct laws, particularly if you are going on a road trip. If driving, be alert to the rules of the road. Some countries will drive on the left side of the road, others on the right.

Luggage

Attempt to prevent baggage changes. More practical is to take a small bag with you in the cabin if your stay is going to be short.

Crime tendencies at destination

This knowledge is very valuable when selecting hotels and the dynamic of the neighborhoods.

Selecting a secure Hotel

Make sure you select it cautiously. If possible get recommendations. Stick to reputable national chain, these tents to have secured personal. Also, try to get one that has rooms that can only be accessed through the interior lobby. This type of hotels requires anyone entering the hotel to walk by the lobby or pass through other locations required to use a room key.

It is also a good plan to select one with a restaurant facility that way you eliminate the need to leave the hotel after dark if you don't feel secure with its surrounding, diminishing your exposure to danger.

Check-in

Under no situations leave your bags unattended, decline the bellman service, visual control is logical, I always place the bag between my feet's while waiting in line.

Some nations require tourist to turn in to hotels, passports, if you worry about this, copy your passport information and a photocopy of the main passport page, to turn in.

Respectable hotel chains must never announce your room # aloud. If she/he does it, respectfully ask for another room and not to call the number orally. This may sound unimportant; protecting your room number is part of controlling your security. Many criminals loiter around lobbies looking for potential victims. Maintain a high-level of awareness every time you go to your room, watch if anyone is following to your room. If necessary, ask an escort to your room.

Immediately inside your room, test the door and the secondary lock. If it has a door that joins to an adjacent room, make sure it is securely locked. Make sure the windows are locked, and take a peek thru the window to see what is there. Also, verify the phone to make sure that it functions properly.

Walk down the stairs, so you see where it is, and where it exits. This is crucial, in case of a fire, likewise if you're evading another emergency and don't expect to end up in the street, a stairs that goes to the vestibule is better.

Many times thugs follow you to your room, talking peacefully with another man or a female, to make you think they are also hotel tenants. You let your guard down, bannn!, right in front of your room the moment you are unlocking your door, they produce a gun or knife, force you inside your room, then inside, they open the doors to others criminals, rob you, maybe rape you if you are a woman. Who knows what else?

Never ever open the door to an unfamiliar person, if someone claims to be a hotel employee, call the front desk and confirm. If the employee needs to do maintenance, tell him/her to come back after you've left the room. If he brings you something, ask him or her to leave it by your door. Uses the peephole to make sure the individual is gone, wait 10 or more minutes, look again, and with caution, open a little bit and removed the article.

ROOM RULES

Request a room nearby by the elevators. Have your key ready when you leave the elevator.

When you make your reservation, ask for a room faraway from an emergency exits.

Emergency door may be used by thugs and rapist to avoid using the elevator.

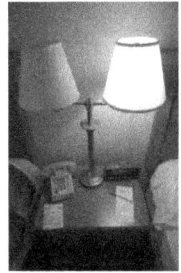

The hotel door should have double locks and a dead bolt with a peephole. Bring along a security doorstop just in case for extra protection.

Hanging the **makeup sign** is an invitation in for crooks. Don't hang up **the please make up** this room sign, this tells everyone you're not there. Call housekeeping instead.

Is a great idea to use the **do not disturb sign**. This would make the room seem occupied, use it.

High-priced clothing must be placed in hangers under other garments if possible. Robbers usually "shop" for what they can't see, the thugs mind figure it out that you hire your best clothes and valuables.

Don't bring any valuables in your trip, if you do, lock valuables in the front-desk safe. Much safer than in the room.

If anything is stolen from your hotel room, tell the administration right away. Most hotel robberies are committed by the staff, and many hotel, especially overseas, don't allow employees to leave with packages, thieves take the money and dump the rest.

Don't forget, when using the elevator stand near the push button with your back to the wall, if threatened push all the buttons at once with your back.

I trick I use when I travel along is to place a piece of furniture against the door, so if someone try to open the door is going to find resistance and I will have time to react to the noise and invasion.

Taxis
Choose hotel taxis when you can. Make sure to look at the car and driver before you get in, make sure it is from a known company, check his credential visually yourself. If you get uneasy at any time get out fast at any corner, use any excuse to get out like you have to throw up if you have to. For a woman, is better not to sit in the front taxi seat, right away check to make sure the doors open from the inside. Have the money ready before you arrive at your destination, do not delay leaving the car.

Never get into a car with a stranger.

Getting Into Your Car...

Walk and stay alert. This is a most. Be alert at all times. Look at the big pictures as you walk to your car, is there anything peculiar happening, like a car on with a guy in it? Is there anything you don't like? Do you fell something is wrong?

Be alert!

Is there anyone just walking around and looking behind his shoulder that appear like to be lost or do not belong there? Or this person is acting weird, like he does not belong. Does he look nervous?

Move toward your car with the key in your hands. Don't waste your time, keep focus, get in and leave.

If it's late at night, dark or lonely, try to walk close by a group of person or a couple, a rapist or a predator from a distance may think you are not alone. If you are really concern, ask them a question, or make a comment, to appeal you have company, separate from them at the very last minute when you get close to your car.
This way from a distance the criminal think you are not alone, he then will look for another easy prey.
Gaze around as you get close to your automobile and look inside the car, especially in the back seat before getting in.

Be careful with people inquiring for directions. Don't get close to them, better off do not answer, or talk to strangers under any conditions, it could be a trick, keep as much space between them as you as possible.

This way they can't force you inside their vehicles without people around seen it.

Keeps an eye for big vehicles obstructing your view and the view of others?
Be alert if someone left the store behind you, if there is somebody, look back for a few seconds, look at the person if you feel uncomfortable turn around and go back inside.

Call someone, a friend a co-worker, somebody even the security to walk you down.

98

If something makes you feel uneasy, get into the car without delay, lock the doors, and drive away, or go back into the store if there is someone between you and your car.

Lock the door and start your car , move and only then when you are in a position that allows you to drive forward , lock your safety belt, or look at your package if you must. I repeat your car should be in a position so you could drive away if you must. This is one of the mistakes I see women doing all the time.

If a criminal is in the car and point his gun to your head do NOT drive off, important: do NOT drive off! Instead, step in the engine and speed into anything, store window, bus, gas station, wrecking the car. The airbag will deflate helping you with the impact. Open the door and run.

You have a much better, chance this way of surviving than if you go with him or them.

Cars and Carjacking

Driving

At traffic how many times you have not allowed anyone from pulling his car pass you and in front of you? How many times have you yielded at a driver because of his driving? How many times you have said to yourself I'm not backing down fighting over a parking space? What or who this guy thinks he is? Those same decisions in today's world and with the wrong person can be fatal.

How many times we heard on the 11.00 pm o'clock news about the same circumstance that was scaled up? Then, we said to ourselves, that situation wasn't worst it. How this ever happens? It was very stupid. That's right, it was stupid. You know what? Most of us at one time or another do something stupid like that, Correct?

On the Road

Leave an adequate amount of space between you and the car in front of you. Always check your mirrors when you stop. Make sure to park in a well-lit and busy area.

Keep your doors lock at all times, windows up in a dangerous area or new to you.
Avoid unfamiliar routes. You could end up on the bad gang neighborhood. Get good instructions always when going somewhere new.

When you stop specially at a traffic light or stop sign, leave enough room to get out around other cars. Do not stop really close to the car in front, in case you need to get away.
Use the center lane, particularly at night or when driving thru a bad neighborhood, it is harder to get to you this way.

You are at a traffic light or any place and a man approach you, you don't have to pull down your window and engage in a dialogue. Assault victims usually feel something is not right in the initial moments they run into their attackers, but were socially held back to take necessary action to leave and escape.

If you're bumped behind by another car, don't get down unless is in a well-lighted place with car traffic or traffic people.
Move to a place where there is traffic and light. If in real doubt situation, **get out of there**, your life, its worth more than fixing your car.

A frequent tactic is someone drives by you and points at your car like telling you something is wrong with it, so you will stop and get out and check. **Don't**

If you get out of the car because of an accident or any reason, stay very attentive and very aware of everything going around you; if possible keep your cellular phone in your hand and ready.

One night a was driving home with a friend when all of a sudden I was bumped behind by another car at a stop sign, I was shocked because I just made a right turn out of a very busy highway, and I was sure that nobody drove behind me. In those particular days there were news on TV that this was being done to rob people. So my friend George, said get out of here don't get out!

That's what I did, but as I drove away, I looked thru my rear mirror and saw the car making a left turn and speeding away with the

Headlights off-It seems to my friend and me that the predator or predators were waiting off the mayor highway waiting for someone to drive by and stop there.

Probably they had been researching the street corners and came to the conclusion that hiring and waiting for a victim, there was an excellent spot for him/them.

Another time I was driving home in the expressway alone about three o'clock in the morning, as I exit out of the freeway I had to stop in a red light. There was nobody around, the exit street was desolated with not too much light, and none traffic at those hours of the night.

As I looked thru my rearview mirror, I saw a car stopping behind me at this light. I found that very strange because at that time is not usual for this to happen. I kept my eyes open, looking behind me through the mirror, when all of a sudden I saw the two door car opened and two men came out running toward me from both sides of the car. I step on the car gas, burn some tire, took the red light, and speed out of there.

I escape for sure of being robbed, or maybe even worse. Lucky I was aware. Three times I have escaped from being the victim in a street driving because I was aware.

The other time I was driving home also about three o'clock in the morning, I was driving a two seated Triumph Spitfire convertible 1983 a classic car. As I approached the exit of the freeway, I saw the car in front of me about 100 or 150 feet in front of me stop, blocking the only exit space in the freeway.

The emergency blinkers come on the car and two men got out of the car and started to walk slowly toward my way. I stop my car pretty far from them, there was no other way to go, but reverse into the freeway, and I saw the situation developing right in front of my eyes. These two guys were approaching me making hand gestures like help me or my car broke down, or at least that is what I interpreted.

Fast I came to the conclusion that this was a robbery. Bet you anything that 99% of the people would have driven forward to see if it there was space to drive thru or to talk to these people. Not me, as they kept walking toward my car I keep running my

101

car in reverse, keeping about the same distance from them since they stop the car. As I was reaching in reverse the freeway very slowly to drive away from there, I saw the two men turned around and ran for the vehicle, got in and drove away at very high-speed. I was scared, shock, but again, my instinct and awareness have paid. I waited a couple of minutes, drove up and out of the freeway, I keep glancing my rear back mirror to make sure nobody was following me. As you can see, they did not have any car problems it was only a trick to fool me.

What a nice plan!!, it's late, nobody around, very dark, think about it, the car in front of your stall in an exit, you drive up to them, and between feet's away from them, they take out a gun and force you to get out and robbed you or worse, force you to take one of them as a passenger while the other follow you behind in the other car. Force you to take money out of many ATM's, or drive them home where they keep you and your family kidnapped while they rampage your home. And who knows, maybe you even lose your life or one of your family members.

If you suspect a tail, keep an eye on the car, make two or three turns to confirm is following you. Signal in one direction, but all of the sudden and quickly turn the other direction. Do not drive home or stop, if you see a police car make some kind of gesture or drive in the police car way and explain your situation.

If you drive thru a busy intersection, slow down to get a yellow /red light, make believe you are stopping, the car following you may get stuck at the traffic light, if a police stop you, better, tell him what, was going on.

Car Accident

If your car is in working condition signed the other car driver to follow you, drive your car to a busy location if the area is desert or dark. Honk your horn so people would look and take notice of what is going on. Be very careful with a situation like this. Drive your car to the next gas station or 24 hours quick food store. If not call on your cell the police right away and tell them where you are, do not hesitate, or waste time.

Many times not only the rapist, but also the criminal/thieve use this trick to stop people so they can attack them.
If you are suspicious, leave right away and call the police from a secure area and explain the situation.

Getting Out Of Your Car

Conceal package or bags left in your car, please do it before arriving at your parking destination, so nobody can tell what you are doing 50 feet away from you, or put them in the trunk.

If you're late, still look around and stay aware of the surroundings. This must become a part of you; you must do it even without thinking.

In a rush you make mistakes and the predator that's what he is waiting for, your mistake. If there is a person walking close by wait a couple of minutes to make space between you and him. Stay alert and if you don't feel comfortable, move on, get out.

Keep your eyes open!

Getting out Of Your Car at home

If you are arriving home special after shopping in the store, market or from the bank it doesn't matter if it is day or night, get into the habit of checking thru your mirror before getting home to make sure nobody follow you. Get into the habit of doing this, once in a while I hear on the nightly TV news that someone was followed home, robe and force into their home, don't let this happen to you and your love one.

The criminal pay attention to the jewelry you wear and the car you drive.

When you are a block or two away from home make a turn if you suspect someone may be following you, make another turn, make sure, make a couple of turns, if the car makes two or three turns after you, drive to a well-lit area, store, restaurant or call the police on your cell if you think you are being follow or in doubt. It's better to be sorry than to be death, rape or hurt.

This is a very serious situation to fall for, it only takes a few seconds to check thru your mirrors and if you suspect anything doing this tactic is only going to take away from you a couple of minutes of your life. Compare to maybe lose your life or someone dear life's in a couple of minutes. Don't neglect this tip. It could save a life.

When entering your home take a fast look at your doors and windows as you approach the door. You should never have big trees or bushes by your door so somebody can hide in them.

Also, if there is anybody walking by your house, close to where you are going to park? Do you know this person? Have you seen it before? Stop! Don't get out, wait for him to leave or just go around the block and come back with your eyes open.

This is a favorite technique of criminals. They get you getting into your house, and then you are their mercy. They even call more people once inside your home. Beware!

Beware!

104

Vehicle Safety tips

A cell phone is a most and one of the best safety devices you can have!
Don't park next to vans or pick-ups because they will obscure you from view and you can be easily forced in by the side door.
Get in first, lock the doors and then organize your personal effects
Don't ever, ever pick up hitchhikers.

If a friend drops you at work or home, ask friends to wait until you are inside your home, or that your car is started and driving before driving away.
Do not label your keys with any information. If you lose it and get into the wrong hands, they can find you.

Don't ever drive with less than a half of a tank of gas. Get use to fill up before this happens. You never know when you are going to need to drive extra at any time.

If you have a flat tire and feel that you are alone at night or in a neighborhood that is not safe. Drive to a place of safety very slowly with your hazard lights on. Buy two of those cans to fix and inflate a tire. They work and only take a couple of minutes. Compare to being stalled on the side of the street for hours.

Never place controversial stickers on your car, including political or mentioning gun.

Try to park in a very lighted or traffic area as you can. Do it fast and get out. Don't waste your time talking on the phone or drinking a soda. Get out!
Never accept a ride, if you must, pick a car driven by women or families are much safer. Less risky.

Auto Theft

Many cars had the airbags stolen out of it right in front of the victim's residence. A friend of mine had his car T-top stolen and as soon as he got them replaced, they came back; of course they knew he had to install new ones. So they already, had an address to visit once in a while. Another friend got his airbags stolen as soon as he got the air bags replaced, they came back. This kept going in circles for a while.

A car is stolen every 25.5 seconds in the U.S., according to the National Insurance Crime Bureau

Tips

Never leave a window cracked open on a parked car, not even a tiniest bit, this is like telling the criminals "steal this car".

Another oversight many people do is they leave an unoccupied car running in many different places like fast food store, gas station, or ATM, this is another bad idea. According to the Department of Transportation's Automobile Burglary and Theft Prevention Authority or ABTPA.

Thieves are always on the lookout in these locations, waiting for such opportunities.

The motive why so many stolen cars are never found is that most of the time these cars are exported to other countries or broken down for parts in chop shops.

Immobilizing Devices

There are a few Immobilizing Devices, some are Kill switches, fuel cutoffs, and some new cars come with a smart key. Think about it, if your car can't run, can't get stolen. Period. Kill switches can be a simple on/off switch or high Tec. You can have a locksmith install one.

Tracking Systems

Satellite-based tracking systems can help law enforcement find and recover stolen vehicles faster than anything else in the market. Many vehicles are being outfitted with these systems from the factory; they require a yearly subscription service and usually cost between $300 and $1,000. If you can afford it is good to have it.

Many will inform the owner if the vehicle has been moved without your knowledge. Third-party systems include LoJack, which emits a signal to police when a vehicle is stolen, and Millennium Plus, which employs GPS and wireless technology to track stolen vehicles. New systems are coming out, but the one mentioned above without a doubt is the best ones.

Use Common Sense

The best and most economical form of defense is to simply lock, roll up your windows, make sure to lock your car and if your car is a convertible, bring the top up. Simple as that.

Out of Sight, Out of Mind

Keep all possessions, including iPod's, cell phones, briefcases, portfolios, store bags and other valuables; anything the robbers may think is valuable out of sight. Many owners come back to their car to find out the windows vandalize broken on their car, because they left a bag or a briefcase in sight and the thieves thought it was valuable.

Don't tempt the thieves.

VIN Etching

Another idea is etch your car's Vehicle Identification Number (VIN) into the glass surfaces. Because all windows must be replaced before the car can be tagged with a fake VIN for resale. This makes the car much less desirable for the thieves.

Park in Attended Lots

Unattended parking areas are desirable for the thieves more than attended parking lot because one motive, auto thieves do not want people that can be witness of their crimes. Unattended parking lots are target many times more than attending lots.

Valet

Don't leave any documents in your car in the trunk or in the glove box. When you give your car key, make sure you don't give them your home key, if you do ,they will find out with the papers you left in the car where you live, you are in big trouble.

They can make a duplicate of your home key while you are eating, and later on having someone breaks into your home. About 99% of the people do not check upon returning of the car, the tires, the spare and the battery, to make sure they're the same as those you had when you parked. Think about what I just told you for a moment. See the picture?

Many times the valet attendant may change your new battery for his old one. Even the spare tire if your matches his. He knows you are in a hurry. Tomorrow is too late, and he knows it.

Car Running Unattended

Seems very stupid right? Well, it's done all the time. Vehicles are frequently stolen at fast food stores, gas stations, ATMs when the driver runs inside and leaves the car running, just for a moment, right? Well, this is the moment a thief could be waiting for. Steal your car easy and fast without a struggle. Thank you.

On cold mornings many times when an owner leaves the vehicle running to warm up. Many vehicles are also stolen. That's easy!

Don't be a target!

Carjackers Places

Crossroads with stop
lights or signs

Garages

Parking lot

Shopping malls

Grocery stores

Stay away from isolated gas pump

ATMs (automated teller machines).
One of a prefer place

Residential driveways
People getting into and out of cars
Highway exit and entry ramps

If they get you by surprise

Give up your car, **Never, I repeat, never leave with them.** Just
throw them your keys, and then get away from the area fast as
possible. Is your car worth more than your life? Call the police right
away.
If you are inside the car **get out** right away, don't give him a chance
to tell you to stay in the car, "don't wait get out'', if you stay your
chances of getting raped, hurt , or kill goes up tremendously.

Increase your Awareness in these unreliable zones:

Gas Stations- getting gas at the pump-perfect place to hijack your car.

ATM-particularly at night

Home Garage-they run behind you to get in before the garage door
closes.

Parking Garages and Lots

Park in areas with cameras and bright lights. These places are especially vulnerable for Car jackers.

Stooping in traffic lights. You are vulnerable when the car slows down to stop, and maybe you are changing station on the radio, or placing a call or texting in your phone, this moment of distraction is what exactly the carjacker is looking for.

If you get surprise, is time to move to carjack options:

A-Attack with the car. Used the car to escape. Hit the attacker even if he is the way of your escape. It is better to clarify to the police or even a jury your motive that to be killed, rape, and maybe torture.

If the car is blocked contemplate this option.

B-If you can, attempt to escape, abandon the car, give up the car, if the car path is block, get out fast by the door away from the carjacker.

If the carjacker just wants the car, it may increase your chances of survival. Move, run, yell, and make noises. Run to a busy intersection, to a store, to a gas station, anywhere where is light, traffic and maybe people.

"The effectively fundamental to protecting yourself is to react instantly and use any part of your body to attack quickly, violently, surprising the attacker".

At the bank

At the ATM be watchful of people standing around, looking over their shoulder, or taking money out and staying around, placing money in their wallets or counting the money.

The same thing inside the bank, most of the time this person is working with another one in a car outside. If you took a reasonable amount of money, he will call the outside person and tell him, the one with the red shirt. That's all, then the outside guy will follow you, and not surprisingly you don't suspect anything because you haven't seen this person. So when you stop home or wherever you are going this person/s would rob you. This is how crooks work.
 Also, if you buy a lot of merchandise at a store. They use the same tactics and if it is late at night much better for them.

In a drive thru ATM, pick one that is in a busy, well-lit street in the front or side of the bank with an unobstructed view; avoid the ones in the back especially at night. When you reach the bank look over the whole place, who is behind you? As you retrieve money glare at your side view mirrors and see if anybody is walking toward you, also if someone is standing close by, think, why?

If at any time you see someone approaching you or are moving to your car, just leave. Don't drive your car all the way to the one in front of you, if you have to get out and move you wouldn't be able to do it, keep **distance** from the car in front and do not drive up until that front car move and there is space to drive out if you see someone approaching you from the back and side of your car.

Don't let a predator move in and surprise you by your window, be **alert**, when you get your money, close the window and move out of the ATM and then and only then place your money and card in your wallet.
Make sure there is always room in front of you to drive forward if you must, this a very **important tip**, make sure there is plenty space to move forward and to leave.

Be careful of peoples standing around

111

Chapter 3- Home Invasion

In my point of view, this is the worst situation. Waking up in the middle of the night by a sound or noise that someone's inside your home! **This is very freighting!**

At two or three AM when you hear a door knock down or a window shattering, you are shocked, scared. Your right to be scared; anyone breaking into an occupied home is a serious offender. Assume that a burglar entering your home is capable and ready to do harm or kill.

The **elderly** are also frequent targets of home invasion crimes. Home invasion robberies can be traumatizing and can easily and quickly escalate into **violence.**

Too many people feel safe around their cars, outside their houses, arriving at home. That' exactly what a car hiker or the criminal is looking for.

Be sure that any felon who invades into your home knowing you're inside it has entered ready to murder you and your loved ones at any moment.

The instant you realize that an invader wants more than your possessions, you must presume it in any home invasion. You must run away, or fight as quickly as you can, before he ties you up.

Obeying in the belief that a sociopath will honor his word is always the incorrect action.
As soon as you get away, he will realize that the clock is ticking before the police arrive.

The delinquent strategy is to dominate you. All of his actions, his intimidation's and promises—are intended to frighten and control you.

Have your cell phone by your nightstands. Do not go looking for the invader, hide, staying hiding implies you won't make any noises, signaling your location. Hide, but be ready to fight if needed.

Don't turn the lights on, you will give away your position, call the police and if you can get away, escape. Let the intruder look and come for you, don't go looking for him.

The exception, of staying in the house is if your children or wife is inside the house with you.
Enhancing security at home is one of the first steps you must do to prevent being a victim.

You must realize if there is more than one invader? And do it fast. They may be looking to rob you.... Things are going to get out of hand if you have a daughter or a wife. What will you do to protect your family? How? Seconds count.

You must think this before it happens, you and I both hope that this will never happen. However if you think what to do before the situation ever comes, you are going to have a chance to survive. Why?

Because you know where you left the telephone, you know witch door to close, where is the best place to hire, by where to flee the house, where you keep your gun or rifle if you have one, etc.

Several recommendations to help you get ready for an intruder in your home

If you think there is somebody in your home, call the police right away—even if you are not positive. It is better to be safe than sorry. Give this information: **start with your address**; in case you get cut off, your name, the exact location of you and your family members; whether anyone is hurt; and if you think the intruder or intruders have a gun or other weapon. **Don't hang up**, most of the time 911 stays connected to the telephone you just call from.

If your house is big enough, you should have a safe room in your house to which you can retreat. This particular room should be equipped with a strong door, deadbolt lock, phone (preferably cell phone), and a can of pepper spray, fire extinguisher, a weapon of some kind, a gun or a rifle.

Extremely important that this room must have a working telephone or even better, a cellular phone in case the land line has been cut so you can contact an emergency dispatcher during a threatening danger encounter situation.

Your last resort should be fighting when all other alternatives have been exhausted, but make no mistake this is a life and death situation. Those first actions you take are crucial...could mean the difference between life-or-death struggle. My advice is, think what would you do, if you heard somebody in the kitchen for example, can you close a door? Can you leave through the back door? Plan some situation in your head.

Share it with your family members. Give them responsibilities, steps to follow if something like this ever happens. Discuss like we will meet by such a door, get out thru a special window, who is going to call the police, Etc.

Official Research verifies that the majority of armed intruders break-in for two reasons:
They don't realize you're there
They assume you to be powerless

When you found out someone has broken into your house. There are physical and psychological changes. Your heart thumps as adrenaline rushes. Your near vision worsens. You may not hear as well. Time

decelerates down. Your fine motor skills will diminish because your body is getting ready for a physical struggle to either fight or run.

Do not turn on the lights if you hear noises or you are looking for an intruder. Doing so gives away your location. Find a place to hide, wait for the intruder to move, or make noises so you know where he or where they are. At the mean time somebody should be calling the police. It is a better idea to stay put instead of going to look for him/them.

114

Most of home invasion is favorable for the criminal; I'm going to tell you why. They are breaking into your house so the they are loaded with Adrenalin, their adrenaline is running very high, they are in the red zone, on the other hand, you are in white, so is going to be very but very hard for you to win over the situation, you have to go thru white, yellow, orange to get to red.

This is why most of the time the offender wins in a home invasion. They know what they are doing, they are spec ting and ready for any confrontation, but you are half sleep, in your pajamas, probably bare footed, shock of what's going on, for all these reason and they know it, this makes you more vulnerable and awkwardness, you are going to be a victim unless you take note and take some precaution measures.
Many burglaries in the homes were made out by young people; some of them don't have remorse at all and won't hesitate to harm you if they have to. Some may even do it for fun, or because they are under the influence of some drugs.

One of their **favorite tactics** is to make noises outside your home, in your car, making the car alarm go off, hitting your mailbox, anything to call your attention. Most people the first reaction they take is, let me go out and see what's going on, this is what they want, why break in when they can get you outside with the door open?

They are expecting you to go out, and they know where you are coming out, they are hiring in the dark, in the bushes, behind the corner wall, anywhere to take you by surprise and force the way in.

How easy? Right? **never go out**, especially at night, these are one of their favorite ways to get inside and these people tell me this tactic always work, especially if there is a man inside because this is a man reaction, to go out and face the problem, but as you can see the criminal use this in their favor.

Robbers sometimes even allege to be the police in order to get people to open their doors. Don't get out, call the police, let them handle it, after all is better to be sorry than hurt.

Windows

Burglars often break in through a window. Consider installing burglar metal bars. Check how a criminal can see in from the outside into your home with your blinds closed.
Sliding or double hung windows should always be property protected with the use of pins or stick bracket.

Windows, glass can be broken. Install a resistant window film and apply it to all ground level windows you think are easy to get in or in a lonely dark spot of the house. This film comes in different sizes and thickness; I think the 12 mil is enough for home security applications.

Shatter resistant film won't keep the glass from shattering, it will stop a trespasser from smashing their path through a window.

Front doors

Your front door is the first site thieves will scrutinize; a beat-up front door indicates that your home is an easy target. The front doors should always open outward, with special hinges that can't be detached from outside. All outside doors need to be heavy-duty, steel. Doors should at least be solid wooden doors.

Locks

When they notice the standard cylinder lock, they go for it. A double lock makes your door more difficult to break and less appealing to burglars.
It is recommended that you installed a deadbolt lock. Metal door is much safety than wood doors.

Keys

Never mark your keys with your name, address or phone number in case you lose it or give it to a mechanic or parking attendance. Never hide keys in obvious places. If you ever lose your keys, have them change the lock and replace right away.

Lights

Your home security stars outside your home. You are not trying to stop the robber here, but make them slow down or leave and pick an easy target.

Burglars don't like lights; lights are deterring to intruders. Try to install motion lights and place them as high as you can so they cannot be disconnected. Motion activated lights are helpful, buy an inexpensive light that use solar power; you can install them without the help of an electrician.

Every entrance to your home should have one exterior light. It helps turn more than one room light inside so an outsider think that you're not alone.

Home Appearance

Your home should always have a lived in look. Leave a car park in front of your home if you go on vacation. Your home cannot look empty while you are on vacation, that's what the burglars are on the lookout for. Use a timer light to go on and off a couple of times especially at night.

Trash

Thrown away boxes and bags of purchases are like an announcement to robbers that valuables are inside your home.

Keep your new electronics box and other purchases inside the garbage container and take it out only on trash pickup day.

Alarms

Think about setting up an alarm system, a security camera . Get a dog if you have a patio so the barking when a stranger approach your house not only alert you but also is a deterrent to the intruder. Thieves know bogus alarm system signs. There are also portable alarms; these are particular best when you travel.

Security Camera

117

Sliding glass doors

Burglars can throw a brick at them, or take off them from its tracks. Positioned a rod behind the sliding door, to make it hard to slide, drill a hole in the top of the door to install a metal pin in it so you cannot lift it out of the tracks. Do you know why? Because this the first place to go.

Unoccupied House

Attempt to make your home like someone's home by turning on a light, a TV or radio to make some noise. Use electronic timers to turn them on and off automatically.

Landscaping

Place bushes and shrubs by windows to create an obstacle to climbing into windows. Make sure they can't be used to hide.

Mailbox

Many mail in your mailbox is a sign that you're out of town and likely to be robbed. Have a friend pick your mail, or visit your post office and stop your mail being delivered for a few days.

Observable Interiors

You don't want burglars to get a peek inside your home, so shut the curtains, and pull down the shades. Especially at night when is dark.

Answering machines

Never reveal your name. Always say, you're occupied not that you are not home. If you are a woman living alone have a male friend record the message. It is a good idea to say **we** instead of me to give the impression that more than one person lives at your home.

> *No sensible person ever opens the door of his house without.*
> *knowing who is knocking*
>
> *Jeff Cooper*

Castle defense

Daytime break-ins

Nighttime break-ins of occupied residences are some of the extreme dangerous crimes; however, it is immensely, dangerous daytime invasion.

Home invasion happens on one of two ways. The assailant breaks in or you allow him to enter ploy of a deception. Not only you must take the necessary precaution, your family must observe the safety rules and warnings suggestions. Most home invaders pose as a salesman, repairman, stranded driver or law enforcement.

One important phase of home security is never divulged your security with anybody outside your family. This includes, keys, security codes, you never know who could repeat this information anywhere else and use it against you. If you drive home and you believe someone has broken in. Rapidly leave outside and call the police, even if you are armed.

Most likely home burglaries happen during the daylight hours when no one is home, many burglars confronted by a homeowner run away, but not all, that is why you need to have an emergency plan and better yet keep a home-defense firearm close at hand.

The first thing burglars will do after breaking into your home is going into to your master bedroom, they search your dresser and your drawers for jewelry, they also check your kitchen drawers, and cabinets looking for any valuable items.

You have to be smarter than them, hide your money, jewelry in a cereal box, or in other similar objects, making it harder for them to steal.

Burglars have declared that an alarm-company sticker on a home makes them choose an easier target. Others claim that knowing which alarm system your home has can help them work to disarm your security alarm. This is extra work, and not all of them know how to disarm it or the time to do it.

Maybe you enter your home and encounter a burglar, this situation has become dangerous, possibly the intruder is going to attack you. Try to rapidly leave the home instead of a confrontation. Of course, if you are attacked, you must defend yourself, but always aiming for the outside door, do whatever it takes, but always aiming to go outside.

People passing by may see it, neighbors may hear the commotion, someone is probably going to call the police, and the intruder will make a run and escape. Inside, with no body witnessing, you could get hurt, kill, or capture. Then, the situation became genuine dangerous.

Keep in mind that break-ins during daylight hours are often very violent. Most of the time they assume to no one be at home, then you are a witness, you become a problem.

If your wife or daughters are inside, or you yourself are a woman, then the situation became explosive frighten.

Think nothing in your home is worth dying for. Your basic strategic choices in the occurrence of a home invasion are1-escape, 2-hide, 3-fight if you must.

Discuss this with your family members, in case of an emergency, where is a good place to hide? If you exit your house to your backyard, where is a good spot to hide? If you leave through the front door how far to run and where to?

Consider that there may be more than one assailant involved. Make sure the person exiting the house first, look out before unlocking the door or window, for other threats before opening.
Citizens must have at least one weapon at home. Home-invaders are crazy enough to take that risk. What are they capable of doing?

Remember; under no circumstances open any door for anyone even if that person appears to be a police. Call 9-1-1 and wait for a patrol car to arrive.

An ounce of prevention is worth a pound of cure.
Benjamin Franklin

Dangerous Home offense Situation

Situation A

This is the most dangerous situation, but less common. The crooks get into your house and take you and your family hostage. They will use force, fear and threat tactics to get money, jewelry or desire property. A woman or young girl is in very dangerous to get raped.

Situation B

The criminals come into your residence not knowing you are there, surprise you, but they too get a surprise, their goal was to get in, take as much property as they could, not get caught, or have a confrontation and a witness. Very dangerous situation, now both, you and they have a bigger problem.

Situation C

The thug or thugs are inside your home knowing no one is inside; you arrive home, open the door and find yourself face- to-face with the intruders. Very dangerous, now you have seen them. Now the situation has changed, are they going to hurt you? Are they going to run away without hurting you? Now you can identify them to the police.

In a situation like this is better to make noise, outside far away from the home entrance giving them the opportunity to leave with no one getting hurt. And call the Police.

Situation D

The best situation, the thieves got into your home unoccupied at the time, you return home and find out evidence of a burglary; everything is upside down, clothes on the floor, drawers open, a mess. You check the house in a hurry to make sure no family member was inside. You call the police.

Existent weapons in a home:

You may think you have no weapons at home in case of an emergency, but you do. Here are just a few.

Fork & knife

Kitchen Cleaner

Disinfectant Spray

Scissors

Broom

Sudden weapon in a garage or yard, here are a few:

Hand Garden

Trowel Shovel

Garden Hose

Machete

Hand fork

Grass Shears

A few samples:

Hammer   Machete   Hand fork   Hedge Shears   Mattock Pick

Safeguard Your Home in Google Map

Is easy, anyone can go to Google Maps and check your home or any home.

You type in any address in the nation and see the house, what kinds of cars are in the driveway. One more action you can take to secure your privacy is to remove your house to be seen in Google Map.

Here's how to hide your home on Google, is very easy.

Go to Google Maps and type in your home address. When your home picture comes out, click the picture, it will enlarge and take up the whole screen.

In the bottom, right corner of this screen you will see the words report a problem. Click on the report a problem; you will be taken to a page where you can request to have your home fade out.

Once you've provided your information, you will get an email that says, Thanks for submitting your Street View report. We're reviewing the image you reported and will email you when your request is resolved.
Check their maps a few days later to make sure they took care of it, otherwise, do it again.

This takes a few minutes to protect your privacy and keeps snooping eyes from seeing what's in front of your house. It's one more tool you can use to protect you from burglars to stalk you.

By failing to prepare, you are preparing to fail.
Benjamin Franklin

My advice

I advise you to spend some money on a house alarm system; your family is worth the expense. If you don't have that money to spend now, do the poor man alarm, just keep some sodas can , half filled with gravel or pieces of rocks and place them, especially at night by the windows handle or window facis (inside the home of course).

This way if somebody tries to break through the window to get inside, the soda can will move and fall to the ground, making an incredible sound in the middle of the night. Enough to wake you and other family members up.

This home device works in two ways , one will wake people up, second, it will scare off the intruder/s, he is going to be shocked and scare because the surprise element for him is gone, in a few seconds somebody in the home will be calling the cops. He or they would be on the run. Your job, of protecting your family was a success!

Comment of on house alarms-The criminal has been known to knowingly set the home alarm off, wait for the police to come by the house and the police make a note that it was a false alarm, when the police leave they go in the house and rob.

This happens in my home a couple of years back, they set the alarm not once, but twice, the police came by the two times. Then, they broke in and this time the police did not show thinking it was a malfunctioning alarm.

The criminal looks a house to rob, they try to pick one with no security alarm, they avoid the ones with good outside lighting if it is at night.

If you hear noises, please get out of bed don't be lazy look into the noise without going out, of course, and do it very caution, and quiet, don't get out of bed running and making all kinds of noises to anticipate yourself to the intruder.
If you don't, you could be in a hostage situation. So investigate.

If you caught an intruder, never take your eyes away from him and his hands. Never talk to him or answer anything, he is trying to distract you.

These individuals are extremely good at disarming strategy. Never get close to him to give him the occasion to disarm you. Call the police at once.

The goal is not to detain the robber, but to safeguard yourself and family. Let him go if you have to, don't go after him either.

Keep in mind that when the attack is gone or stopped so is your rationale for self-defense. If you happen to arrive at home and realize someone has been in the house, get out fast and call the police, let them check the house and find out if anybody still in the interior. I know your first reaction is going inside and find out yourself right away. **Don't**

If in doubt call the police

Home Security conclusion Tactics

Keep **hedges** and small **bushes** short, so the doors to your home are not concealed by any.
Keep entrances well lighted it

Install a **burglar** alarm system. Make sure to display the alarm **stickers** on your windows.

Post "Beware of Dog" signs outside your home.

Install **deadbolt** locks on all exterior doors.

Windows must be **locked**, keep them locked while out or home.

Secure sliding doors, with wooden or metal rods. Many patio doors can be open by picking up and disconnecting the door.

Make sure your house front door has a **peephole**. Or install them.

Repeat every day or every time you have a chance to your kids not to open doors to **strangers.**

Your phone number should be unlisted or use only your **first initial** in your telephone listing.

Never **admit** to an unknown caller that you are by yourself in your house. Tell them that your husband, son, friend is asleep, or in the shower.
Keep fences lock all the time.

Very helpful to have a phone by your bedside. Keep police number phone, fire, friends or family members close by your bed, not by the kitchen.

A **cell phone** is much better in case the criminal cut the lines.

Never said you are **"Not Home"** on your answering machine. Instead, use the term "Unavailable".

HOME

Don't reveal by leaving a message on the door saying you're not at home.

Write your last name and first initial only on your door, mailbox and in the phone book.

When you move to a new house or apartment, switch the locks.
Pull the shades once is nighttime, never dress in front of windows.

Another dead giveaway? Parking permits

Work parking permit- now the delinquent would know where you work.

Apartment parking permit- now the felon would know where you live, when you come out of your house every day, and when you return.

Think about this.

Outside lighting is a very important factor in home security

Placing an emergency call conclusion Tactics

When the police respond the phone call do not hesitate, talk first right away, state your location and name first in case you are disconnected. Tell them why you are calling. If possible answers any questions.

keep **repeating your address** and hire the phone if you have to without hanging it up, so the police can trace your address.
This is a must, do whatever it takes **not to hang up the phone.**

A stranger Knock at your door

Don't open the door to strangers. How many times the TV news is going to tell you?

This is a famous trick; you heard it in the news all the time. The crook specially fools senior citizens and young kids.

They use all kinds of tricks; they claim to be the cable man, the water meter reader, the new mailman. My car broke down the street; may I use your phone? All kinds of tricks don't fall for any.

If in **doubt call the police**, the Water Company or Telephone Company. However, never ever open the door, no matter what they are telling you.

If somebody knocks at your house, look through the pinhole, or by the window, no matter what, if you don't know the person, don't open it. It does not matter if you come out looking rude, it's OK, I'll rather be rude than kill, hurt, or robed.

Some experts in the subject said that if you are alone don't even answer. Others said is better to tell them (of course with the door closed) my son is taking a shower and my brother or husband is sleeping, come back tomorrow. Very helpful to have a phone by your bedside. Keep police number phone, fire, friends or family members close by your bed, not by the kitchen.

Don't talk to them anymore or don't answer any questions. Why? because at times they knock to see if the house is empty.

So if you don't answer, they may try to break-in thinking nobody is home.

Remember, if you don't know the person don't feel bad, just do not open the door, this action could save your life or the life of a love one. If you have any doubts, **call the police!**

Never ever open the door to estrangers!

Outside Safety tips

Late at night there is much less traffic and a predator has a better opportunity of mugging you without being seen or caught.

If you walk, pick a well-lit street with high witness traffic. Walk at all times on the side of the roadway facing traffic. Much safer this way, if a car stops to approach you and you keep walking it has to drive in reverse.

When riding the bus, sit near the driver. Try to sit in an aisle seat.
If you go out to jog on your own, don't wear headphones. If you do, someone can sneak up behind you and you won't be able to hear it. Don't try shortcuts.
If you are not familiar with an area, you may get lost, or get into a dead end street.
Your keys must be ready while approaching your house or vehicle or even while walking your dog.
Never displays money in public. When in an automatic teller machine take your money and hired right away. Don't count it in public Always try to keep one hand free when carrying bags.

IF SOMEONE FOLLOWED YOU

Never go home. Stop at a Firemen Station, grocery store, fast food restaurant and call the police or your boyfriend, friend or anybody. Tell him loud to stop bothering you, the point is for everybody to find out and look and be aware of the situation, probably after this he will leave fast out of there and leave you alone, since he don't want people to see him.

If someone followed you walking and it is kind of lonely and you fear for yourself, begin striking or bump into parked cars in your way as you walk to set off cars alarm, remember most people won't go out to help you out of fear, but if you throw a rock or something thru a window is another history even if you pay later for the damage and explain the circumstances to the authorities, is a wise and smart action to take compare to your life or being raped.

If you decide to run be sure to run to a store or business that you are sure is open, you don't want to use your energy for the wrong situation or move. If he followed you and there is no place to hire, you are wear out and a much less disadvantage situation than before.

A Point to remember –fight back right away without hesitation, don't waste time and if you must fight, fight in the street in the open. This will surprise him or those, people are most likely to see it and somebody may help you or call the police right away.

Stalking

Report shadowing right away to the police.

Keep records of all incidents.

Do not try to talk with the stalker.

Tell everybody about these circumstances, friends, family, co-workers.

Consider about getting a restraining order.

Walking Suggestions

Wear clothes typical for your localities.

Stay in well-lit areas.

Avoid parking close to bushes.

Avoid shortcuts.

Don't accept rides with strangers.

If somebody pursued you on foot, cross the street, go to a well-lit store or go into a home with an intense light, and call the police. If you're being chased by someone in a car, move in the contrary direction or go up a one-way street the opposite way.

The home outside light should always be left on.

Avoid talking on your cell phone when walking.

Do not text message while walking.

Public Transportation

Unfortunately there are many cases of assault occurring in public transit.
Make a point to always seat as close to the driver as you can. Stay away from the rear.
If you are alone, it is wise not to sit by the window so you won't be locked in if someone wants to touch you or bother you, so you can move easily at any time

Trust your instincts.

Get there just a few minutes before the bus or train, so you do not have to wait alone long.
Never sleep in the bus/ train, I repeat, never ever sleep on the bus or train.

Stay away from dark lonely stations

It is much better and wiser to use busier stops when possible.
If someone makes you uneasy, move away. Walk in the direction of the crow, or where is a lot of people.
If someone harasses you, do not be afraid to make a scene.
The driver is responsible for keeping order, beside once people see the person who is molesting you, this person don't want to be recognized later. He will stop, or probably leave the bus/train.

Same when riding the subway, seat in the front car.
Plan your route ahead of time. Know where you are getting on and off.
Keep alert who is getting off, with you.
If someone that worries you get off with you, walk into a store, gas station or any place and check again to make sure he is not following you.

132

Self-defense Techniques

Self-defense to be helpful does not have to require physical peak, top fitness level or maximum flexibility. Self-defense has to be reliable no matter your condition, age, size; otherwise it would not be practical.

When thugs confront you, you should be in a ready position. Never directly facing him, your body should be at an angle to the aggressor. Keep your hands close to your chest, try not to appear aggressive. Never place your hands, in your pants pockets. Keep your eyes on him and his hands. Make sure to keep at arm's-length, try not to be in a crowded spot or situation, this way you can move to any side if you need to.

No matter how huge the attacker is, this course of action must be suitably applied by men or women!
For defense, practice one or two techniques that you feel comfortable with, is much better, to be able to execute two fast techniques, quickly and with authorization than half-know 50 techniques.
You will need to faint or fake your defense, finger stabs into his eyes, use the forearm and elbows, specifically under the nose, hit him under the last rib, the Solar Plexus, groin, knees, and shins. No matter how huge or physically powerful an attacker is he has vulnerable areas, especially the ones mention above.

Yell-Scream

Yell or shout, the effects of a loud noise can reduce your attacker for a brief moment at the same time you are calling attention to you and your situation. Yelling is a great street defense. Most of the attacks are done by bullies; remember they are looking for victims not adversaries. It will help you exhale and it won't harm you as bad if you get hit in the abdomen because you just exhale the air, it distracts and confuses your attacker and makes you a little faster. So yell!

Move

If you can, move, move all-around; move your hands in circular motion, up and down, this will confuse the attacker at the same time use as a blocking defense. However, always away from the predator or forward where there are people or car traffic or a spot with a better lighting.

For defending yourself, pick a couple of basic techniques, then practiced over and over, every time you recall, before taking a shower, walking your dog.

In a karate school they instruct many different techniques and most people move on to the next one without really learning them well. So what is best for self–defense? Half -knowing 50 techniques or knowing two that you can apply over and over, fast and with confidence. Think about it. The two that you pick and practices are the one that will help you survive.

Goal

Your objective is to keep yourself from harm, escape, to remain safe is the most important issue.

Hit first

You are facing a dangerous criminal, and no way to escape, you must hit first, strike fast, this is very important to survive a street confrontation, but do it as a last option, when there is no other way out. Striking first is the best way since you are using the surprise element. It will give you the upper hand because of the abruptly and unexpectedly attack.

If you allowed your attacker to hit you with the first strike is stupid. You probably be hurt, injure or maybe he will kill you with that first strike.

Make sure when using force that is necessary and a really dangerous situation.

Be aware of that there is Lethal force; this is when you cause bodily injury or death. The other is Non-lethal force, and does not cause serious bodily injury or death.

Here you have to be concerned, if you act with serious force against your aggressor; you could deal with the official prosecution later. If you are attacked, it is better to try to prove your circumstances later than to get hurt, or even get killed.

This is why the rationale behind de-escalate situation is crucial. Here is where the situation turns out to be complex. Usually for defending yourself, you should hit first, but here is the problem, witness can testify they saw you hit first and under the law you could give the impression to be the aggressor.

Keep in mind that de-escalation a conflict not always work, frequently it backfire, and makes the crook more violent.
Fighting back is not for everyone. Situations are different, and not everyone is the same, the decision to run, hide or fight it is up to you.

Striking first must be your last result, from the point of view of the law you could be sue, arrested, etc. Make certain this is the only way to save yourself.

Of course in a life or death circumstances, you don't even have to think about it, your life or the ones you love should come first, especially when you are a law obeying citizen and your attacker probably has a long criminal record.

High Kicks

Don't do high kicks in actual fights because you are going to lose your balance for sure and go down. This is done in the movies all the time, but in real life is hard to use because you have to be in top shape, young and have been practicing a lot. High kicks take much more skill and training so for self -defense is discarded.

Low kicks

If you are going to use any kicks at all, use low kicks, to the shin, groin or ankles, low kicks are safer to do and much easier to learn, and you don't have to spend hours practicing them.

Brain

Your most effective weapon is your brain. You are going to be really nervous. However, your attacker, too. Use your most powerful tool, your brain.

Escape

Do you have a way to get away? Back doors, hire, anything to stop the attack, do anything in your power to flee, get out of the situation as fast as you can, do whatever it takes to get you out.

Do

Look up and to the attacker, stand up straight and tall, don't take your eyes away from him, especially from his hands where he may have or hide a weapon.

Do

If he asks you for your money or watch, give it to him or better off, throw it to him from a distance, so you don't have to get close to him.

Distract him

Only if the state of affairs is getting worse, tell him I hear the police, do you? This is going to make him nervous and run off; he does not want to get caught because he is nervous and in the critical situation may believe that you really heard it and he did not. Do not use this method if the predator is walking away or leaving the scene.

Don't

Negotiate with something he can take anyway, if some family member is in life or death situation you may try some kinds of negotiation just to gain time. Never take him home where he can kill you or rape somebody. Never get in a car with your attacker.

Fist strike

Have you ever guessed why boxers tape their hands and on top of that they wear gloves? Easy justification is because if you hit someone with your bare fist, probably you are going to fracture yours fingers or your wrist. Even with all those precautions boxers sometimes break their wrist or fingers. That is why is better to strike someone into their eyes with your fingers or with the palm of your hand.

If you must

If you have to protect yourself go after their eyes, throat, stomach, groin, no matter how strong he is, these parts are very vulnerable.

Fundamental concepts

Make full use of any weapons on hand, sticks, bottles, car antennas, car keys, writing pen, pieces of wood, pencils, hair pin, **anything.**

Maneuver, move, and push, bump, Try to move to a busy street or a better lighter place. Yell, scream, make noises, a lot of noises, yelling and screaming as loud as you can. Get out of the situation as fast you can. Do not stick around.
Your goal is survival and escape as soon as possible.

Violence is my last option.
Chuck Norris

True Equalizer a Gun

The only **true equalizer** is a **gun**, but the gun topic is beyond the scope of this book, many people do not want to carry a gun for various reasons.

Religious, safety, if they have small kids, they are afraid to have a gun at home or carry one, others think they can hurt themselves and others think that having one most likely will escalate the situation.

The only way to stop a bad guy killing people with a gun is a good guy with a gun who is prepared to defend him/her and innocent.

We all know the controversial concern, there is about guns. Some citizens believe the constitution gave the people the right to bear arms, while another belief they should be eliminated.

That's why we won't get into the gun subject in this book. Decide for yourself about the subject of owning a gun.

If you decide to own a gun you must take responsibility.

Always assume that is loaded.
Never ever pointed at anyone
Keep them away from children's
Never place your finger on the trigger unless you are ready to use it
Always secure your gun with a safety lock especially if you have kids at home

Practice, practice, practice to learn and get familiar with your weapon. Talk to your children and teach them the danger of gun. What to do if they find one. I personally taught my daughter and son how to shoot and handle a revolver when they were very young. This way, if they ever found a gun the curiosity to investigate was not there.

As a parent, you are responsible to keep guns out of kids' ways, in a safe unreachable place and with a safety lock.

There are two kinds of guns

Revolvers and semiautomatic. Most experts, including myself consider a revolver the best handgun for defense.

The semiautomatic-the main advantage of the semiautomatic is you can load it very fast and also carries more rounds (bullets) anywhere from nine to 16 or more.

The revolver- Carries five or six bullets. Semiautomatic guns sometimes jam, this happened to me in a serious danger situation. That is why I recommend the revolver. There are two kinds, a single action and double action, in a single action revolver the hammer must be pulled back for a shoot to be fired, the double action you just pull the trigger. A revolver does not jam, if a cartridge doesn't shoot; press the trigger again for another shoot.

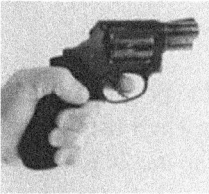

A.38 special revolvers, double action tend to be favored by many experience people because they find ease of use desirable, especially for home protection under stressful situations. If you ever in a situation and you need to neutralize an assailant, find out his intention, you must act before he ties you down or hurt you. Use verbal distraction. Ask him a question, example, did you ask me a question? Where are we going? Distract him a few seconds before you attack him, you are going to have a few seconds when he answers you. Use it!

If you hold a criminal at gunpoint, stay far from him, don't talk to him, and don't answer questions. Don't take your eyes away from him. Ask him to lie down in the floor with arms and legs spread, don't get **close** to him under any **circumstance**. Ask somebody to call the police as soon as you can, tell them the kind of weapon you have, a gun, knife, whatever so when they arrive they won't confuse you with the assailant.

Criminals preferred places to disguise weapons.

Newspapers	Socks
Paper bag	Belts

Revolver

Semiautomatic

A true equalizer is a gun

Shotguns are great for home self-defense. Experts say the sound of a pump action cycling can have a frightening result on thugs.
The eminent noise of cha-chunk of a round actuality loaded to the chamber of a pump-action shotgun is an oh shit! Sound, no delinquent wishes to hear.

For home defense at close range it is hard to beat the 12 gauge shotgun. It is better to use bird shoot instead of slugs, so it won't go thru walls and hit a family member on the other side.

Only concern, issue is the recoil. Fragile, disable people, young kids and the elderly can't; handle the recoil. That is why I recommend the Revolver. There are other shotguns versions like the 20 gauge or 410 which are easier on your shoulder with less recoil.

The 20 gauge is a much easier to handle and a good idea in case your wife or young kids need to defend themselves if you are incapacitated.

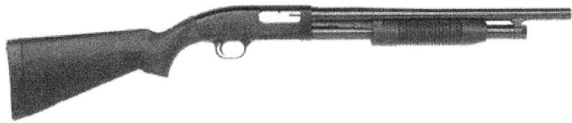

Maverick Security 88-12 Gauge

"The only thing that stops a bad guy with a gun is a good guy with a gun."

Wayne LaPierre

Self-Defenses Lessons

It is unfortunate that today's self-defense lessons are missing real situation confrontations. The intention for this self-defense segment is to present teach or guide you with basic skill that gives you a simple response to some self-protective circumstances.

If you must defend yourself you should know or have an idea of the following:

Timing-
When to strike

Use of feinting-
Deceiving, misleading techniques

Proper application-
Shorts punches, strikes, pushing, pulling, holding, turning, biting and choking.

Exact locations –
The most exposed part of the body to attack

Motion-
Each and every move you make for self-defense should be fast. Automatic, and spontaneous.

Importance should be placed in aggression
This is what is lacking the most in my view in self-defense classes today.

Some knowledge-
Vital areas and organs vulnerable to attack should be learned. In an emergency, you should use your hands (open or closed) feet, knees, elbows, forearms, and head, tapping, poking or striking the attacker's eyes, face, nose or throat.

Courage is knowing what not to fear.
Plato

Chart 1

From Neck up

1-Nasal bone

2-Temple

3-Trachea

   (Wind Pipe)

4-Ear

5-Adam's Apple

6-Lips

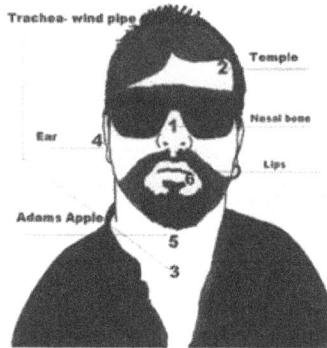

Chart 2

Middle section of the body-Front view

1-Adam's Apple

2-Trachea-wind pipe

3-Heart

4-Solar Plexus

5-Lower Rib Cage

6-Floating Ribs

7-Lower Abdomen

8-Testicles

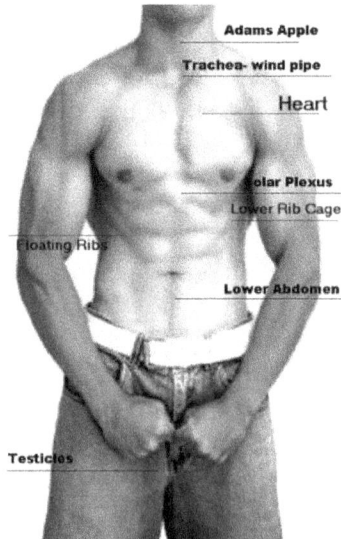

142

Chart 3

Middle section of the body Back view

1-Base of Cerebellum

2-Seven cervical Vertebra

3-First Thoracic Vertebra

4-Seven Thoracic Vertebra

5-Liver

6-Kidneys

7-Tailbone

8-Lower Outer Thigh

9-Inside Knee

10-Base of Calf

11-Achilles Tendon

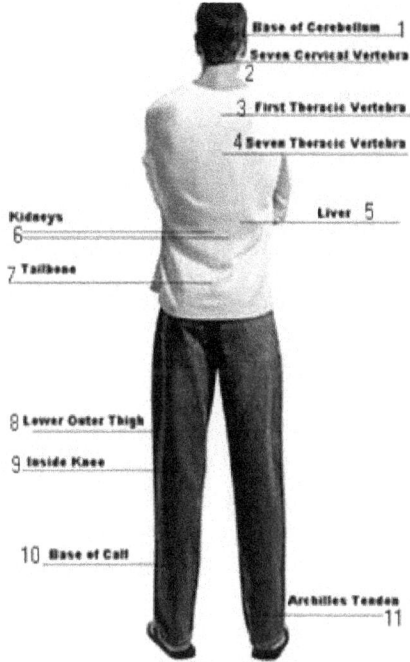

Chart 4

Lower body from legs downside view

4-Knee Cap

5-Shin Bone

6-Instep

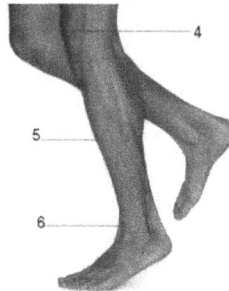

Where and how to strike

Temple blow-is delivered with the inside soft tissue part of the fist, the blow is delivered very fast and to the temple.

The bridge of the nose-strike with the inside fleshy part of the fist, hit down onto the bridge of the nose.

The ear blow-with your close fist and the inside flesh part deliver a strong blow.

The base of the nose-strike up and under the nose. You can use the base of your palm with open hand.

The Solar plexus blow-fast with the fist, can be fatal if you get hit **very** hard.

Spleen blow
To be used for self-defense this blow needs to be delivery very hard.

Strike to the Jaw- Front elbow, nose, or temple.

The Windpipe-or Adam's apple-a heavy blow here could be fatal, you can hit with your open edge side of your hand, with a fist or using the hand like a **"Y"**. You could also reach for the Adam's apple; get a hold of it and pull let out.
This technique is very dangerous, you could kill the predator. Use in extreme situations.

The base of the skull blow-a strike here is very possible to cause injuries.

The throat hollow blow-this blow is delivered with fingertips into the hollow at the base of the neck.

Under the last rib blow-striking this area with open hand fingers cause strong pain.

The Groin blow –unless you are very closed to your attacker this technique should not be good to use. If you are in close range of the attacker you could be facing the criminal or if he have a hold of you from the back, grabbing or hitting is very effective if you can hit the groin.

Abdomen blow- a blow hard enough here can cause a lot of pain to the predator.

Shin blow-very good defense to hit here, this bone is very sensitive.

Ankle blow-good for defense.

Kidney blow-very vulnerable spot. Very good defense if you strike this area.

Finger stabs-This blow is only good to be used on soft areas of your attacker. The use of the fingertips under the jaw or into the eyes is very, very effective.

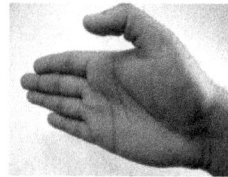

Hand Blow- close fist –open hand, depends on the situation, you could strike the attacker with an open hand for example into his eyes, in the windpipe, or with the closed fist with the fleshy side like to the temple.

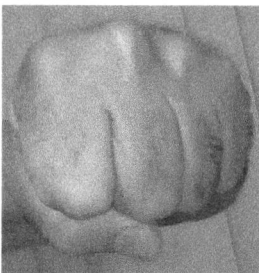

The chances of breaking your fingers or wrist are quite high with fist strike. Fingers tightly squeezed together and jabbed full-force into someone's eye will do more to end a fight than most people's fist punching. Kick to the groin or head butts are much safer and powerful than your fist.

Elbow strike-Use the elbow in an upside movement to hit the chin, the eye or the nose. If he is behind you strike into his solar plexus, or into the abdomen, if he is in front the elbow strike can be straight upward, or the elbow in a circular motion into his nose, jaw. The elbow is the strongest point on your body. If you are close enough to use it, do!

145

Knee blow-use in close encounters, when you are holding against the attacker in a front hold situation. Repeat, repeat, repeat the attack, and keep trying as long as he is holding you in a front embrace.

Ground front pins-If you are lying down and he is sitting on top of you around your waist. Do not wait, this is a very dangerous situation to be, head butt him fast, bite him, move your legs up and down to make him lose balance, you must move quickly before he really pin you down.

Against a wall or a car-Go for his eyes, ear, groin, again, you must move quickly, this is the trick to get out, move before he really gets a choke on you.

Head Butting-This is used by most of the street punks, strike the face, nose with the top of your head. This technique is great to use in close defenses. You could also strike back with the back of your head if he is holding you from behind.

Finger technique-The small finger is the weakest finger so your attack should be concentrated in this finger if possible. Bend it backwards hard as you can go for, breaking his finger if you must, so he can release the hold on you. Remember this is not a technique to stop an attack just one more weapon for you to use.

Action expresses priorities.
Mahatma Gandhi

Defense Tips

Nose Blows: Into the nose blows are very effective. Use the palm of your hand, the fist, the elbow in an up or side way strike. Up under the nose is a good defense, especially if you are very close to your attacker

Windpipe-Use this technique if you are in a real danger situation. Strong defense technique.

Eyes- Ideal for self-defense, because they are hard to protect. Poke scratched them from different angles, excellent self-defense technique.

Nails-can be used for gouging and clawing the eyes.

Groin: Excellent attack in close combat.

Temple: Excellent place to hit.

Ear: Remember the champion Boxer? Hit or bite the ear, if you must, uses this technique.

Fingers: If he has a hold on you, go for his pinky fingers, break it if you have to, and don't forget the eyes.

Shin: Perfect place to kick, over and over.

> *The proper course of action, when under attack, is usually to counterattack.*
>
> *Jeff Cooper*

In the Ultimate Moment (Only if you must)

Defenses Techniques for close-up action

Defense against Front Attack
The attacker, as grab you from the front, pinning your arms to your side.
Defenses #1 kick him in the shin, keep doing it, #2-Hit him with your forehead fast and hard. As soon as he releases you, hit him in the eyes with open fingers, run.

Front defense Choke
The criminal gets a grab of you, and he is choking you from the front
 Clasp your hands together interlacing fingers, fast and quickly raise your arms up with all the strength you have, is done like a punch not like raising your arm.
Your arms should now be in a high position, from here follow thru and hit him in the nose or face with your clasped hand. All in one motion, close hands, hit them up, and right away hit him.

Defense Back Attack
Finger Choke Defense
He surprises you from the back, and grips your throat with his fingers. Pull sharply both of his little fingers because they are not used in choking, making them easy for you to grab, bending them back , if you act fast you may dislocate his fingers or broken them.
However, any other finger will do too.
Turn around fast as soon as he releases you, use the "Y" blow to his Adam's apple. Or hit him with open fingers, or fist, run.

Front Grab under Arms
The attacker grips you around the waist with your arms free
1- Kick if you can several times in his shin. .
2 - Clasp your hand together interlaces your fingers and strikes him in his nose or face with your elbow blow. Hit his eyes, temple or nose, and get out
3- Kick his shim, or hit him in the solar plexus or abdomen using your elbows.

Rear Grab under Arms

The attacker grips you around the waist from behind. Right away-fast bend-over-grabs his foot or pant. Pullover with all your strength-fast.

Head Lock Defense

The criminal has affected a headlock from the front. Grip his wrist and jerk down, kick him on the shin and give him a fist blow into his abdomen or fingers into the eyes, or attack his Adam's apple.

Rear Arm Head Lock

You are under a rear choke with the attacker's forearm on your neck. Give him a backward head butt, with all your strength, move a little bit to the side and hit him backward in the groin using your open palm or grip and squeegee.

Gang attack

If you are held from behind by one of the attacker, using the criminal behind you for support kick into the front attacker once he is in range, jump a little bit and the same time hit hard with a back head strike the one holding you in the back. Turn around and yelling, strike one in the eyes or into the Adam's apple. Holds one of the attacker shirt or sleeves since you are holding him you are restraining him to hit you.

Get out and run!

All these defenses techniques should be applied right away to be effective, **the moment he grabs you, you react.** Don't wait for a few moments to find out what he was going to say, or do. It will be too late. At the beginning of the contact, there and then your reaction defense should be applied; seconds later when he has a really tight and strong hold on you will be too late.

Striking first

It is strategically important to strike first, but also keep in mind that if you ever had to go to court this could work against you, if the witness testifies you struck first. On the other hand, if you wait for him to strike you first he could kill you or permanently injured you.

Courage is fear holding on a minute longer.
George S. Patton

149

Distance

Keep your distance as much as you can from your likely attacker, by doing this, you have more defensive reaction time in case he attacks you.

Yelling

Your voice is an extremely and powerful weapon. Yelling can for sure distract a person and be used to surprise. Yelling can also be used to psych out your attacker.

Compound attack

This is a series of combination of two, three even four body strike launched rapidly one after the other, even if one or two misses its target.

Teeth

The teeth can be used for biting any part of your attacker's body, like his nose, throat, ears even finger or his forearms.

There is a very special apprehension with biting, the risk of contracting AIDS.

Speed

You must strike with speed. Chose a couple of techniques and practice it over and over and focus in retracting your punches or strikes as quickly as you can.

Power

Power is the force you generate when you hit an object. Remember moving your shoulder into your blows generate power. Do it.

Timing

It is the ability to perform a defensive drill at the right moment.

Balance

Balance is the skill to keep your equilibrium standing still or moving. You should practice once in a while, walking with your eyes close for a few seconds around your home.

The Author still practice everyday in 2018.

Practice
When you practice the combinations of your choice you must practice ambidextrously, meaning with both hands.

Killer instinct

This is a deadly power hiding inside each of us and is a natural inherent instinct to fight from our ancestor. The power or energy that comes to help us in a life and death situation is called killer instinct.

Your voice

You must maintain control of your voice. Your voice should always be in command.

Too late

The expert said that if you don't see the attacker before he attacks you, it is too late. One of an essential awareness you must develop or pay attention very close is your hearing.

Income level

The type of criminal you may bring attention to depend in many different specific facts.

Are you rich? Wealthy? Do you flash money or jewelry? What kind of car you drive? Your clothes? What kind of watch you wear? Shoes? Purse? All this detail is the one the criminal or predator pay attention to. Of course an older or weaker person is more vulnerable, as are a pregnant woman or a woman with a toddler.

Evaluate

You must learn how to identify, evaluate people, places and actions. You must also keep in mind the location.

Fight back

Means using all you have to defend yourself, your only option is it fight back, sometime your life is on the line. Trust your instincts. If something bothers you or is out of the ordinary almost certainly is.

Self-defense environment

You must evaluate your environment in an attack situation, parking lot, your house bedroom, your car, elevator, public bathroom.

There are special factors to keep in mind, like escape routes, windows, doors, alleys, stairs fences, and any escape route you may think of.

Terrain conditions like if you are standing in the snow, on ice, if it is raining. Would you be able to escape under these conditions?

Behavior

Is he drunk? High on drugs? Breathing fast? Is he using profanity?

Objective

What does he want from you? Robbed you? Sexually assault you? Harm you? Wants your car keys? If you are a woman a rob can become a rape very fast.

Create difficulties for the criminal

Anything you can place between you and your aggressor, automobile, fences, threes. The list could include many objects.

Sudden Weapons

Pretend a mugger attacks you, in school, or at the mall or at work, and you don't possess any weapons, nevertheless you can protect yourself; there are many options of improvised weapon everywhere.

Here are some.

1-Metal Pen
2-Fork-Spoon
3-Umbrella
4-Car Keys
5-Computer Keyboard
6-Ruler
7-Baseball Bat
8-Rolled up magazine
9-Household spray Bleach-disinfectant
10-Kitchen knives
11-Food Tray
12-Soda bottle
13-Soda can
14-Perfume spray
15-Cellular Phone
16-Pencil
17-Scissors
18-Belt
19-Store hangar
20-Comb-brush
21-Stapler

A basic pen in your cliquish fist with one end exposed can be used to strike critical areas, such as his eyes, throat, groin, and neck. You strike not once, but three or four times, fast, one after the other strike. Strike the legs if he is embracing you from behind, yelling as loud as you can.

The keys, everybody carries a set of keys. They could be an effective weapon. When you are walking to your car, holding them appears normal, but additionally you hold a crushing weapon, quick to be used as a weapon, to surprise an attacker, grasp your keys and let a few keys protrude over your fingers, force them against your knuckles in a firm hold. Leave sufficient of the key in your hand for control.

This weapon is used in an extreme close-contact defense. Use gashing motions to your attacker's face, including eyes, throat, groin to create stinging and intense pain, Again, not once, but as many times as you can, yelling loud as much as you can.

These two techniques could save your life; he may temporarily stop his attack because of the surprise, pain, or both, giving the opening to escape.

A Cellular phone after you dial 911 is a perfect weapon to strike the nose, eyes or temple.

A newspaper or magazine roll up can be used as a weapon to strike the eyes.

Last resort for a woman is a perfume spray, sprayed a couple of times right in the eyes.
There are many options for personal defense all around you. All it takes is a perceptive eye.

Spur-of-the-moment Defenses

Hot liquid, Coffee, Tea, hot Chocolate, can be tossed onto the attacker's face, giving you some time to run, or fight back grasping the occasion.
Remember that also cold liquid would give the attacker an instant short discomfort, giving you the unexpected surprise important for self-defense.

There are countless improvised weapons you can think off, look around you, you can find them anywhere.

Peace is not absence of conflict; it is the ability to handle conflict by peaceful means.

Ronald Reagan

Simple weapons

Flashlights, bottles, Baseball bats, chairs and umbrellas and many others like trash can lid.

Distract weapons

Any weapon that can be throw at the predator like car keys, books, coffee, trash cans, chair, anything to gain time.

Armed or unarmed

Does he have a weapon? Are there more than one weapon? Does he is wearing a big loose jacket capable of concealing weapons? Can you see both of his hands?

In a hostile situation never, I repeat never drop your hands to your side and never ever put them inside your pocket.

We can never be certain of our courage till we have faced danger.
Duc Francois de La Rouchefoucauld

The Author doing Sprints in 2018

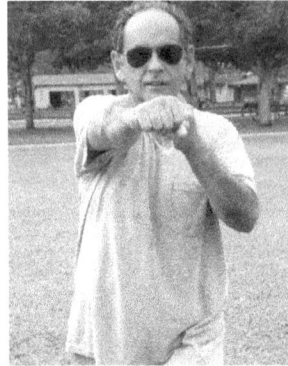
The Author Practice 4 days a week

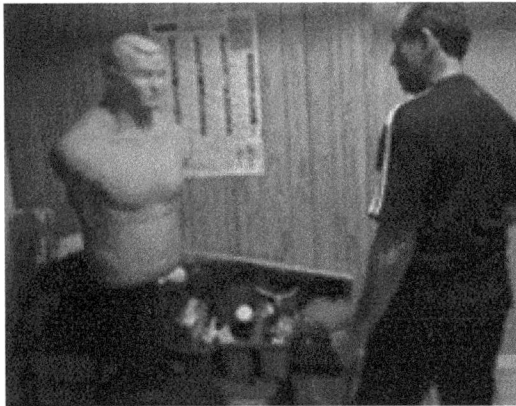

The Author still practicing with the Punching bag after 52 years!

The less effort, the faster and more powerful you will be.
Bruce Lee

Chapter 4-Jogging, Biking or walking the dog safely

Don't go walking/jogging with a Walkman, anyone can tell you are not paying attention. Everybody can tell that you won't be able to hear if a criminal approaches you. Know open stores or places in the area that you can go in an emergency.

Don't ever take the **same route**. Change it. It keeps predators from discovering a pattern in your routine. I know a lady that used to jog every morning at the same time, same park, and same route. Someone waited for her and forced to go to an ATM and take money out, despite the many times I asked her to change her route. She was lucky that she did not get raped or killed.

You must also think that if you ever be confronted by a vicious dog never turn and **run**. You will trigger the "hunting instinct" in the dog if you run. In a low, strong, firm voice say, "No! Stand still, do not look into his eyes, and "Keep repeating "no! no! And wait as long as you have to. Soon the dog will walk away.

Be alert in public restrooms and check the stalls when you enter and use the closest to the door. If you are using the stall and someone suspicious walks in, make believe you are using the phone and said very loud where you are and make sure to say come by for me I'll wait at the door. This way the intruder criminal or not, thinks that someone close by is coming by any minutes now, big chance he will leave and look for another victim.

No one, including this book can tell you what you should do (or should have done) in every situation. You can only make the judgment action for your situation yourself. If you decide to fight-or not. If you decide to fight, make sure you fight harder!

Running Awareness

Most of the time runners are out alone, at odd times, and in lonely places. This can become dangerous if you become careless.

Safe Running

You must be **alert** and **aware** all the time. Why choose a lonely pad when you can pick another pad not so lonely?
If you ask someone who has been a victim, they always say the same: "I never saw it coming" and "It happened so quickly". Awareness, like any other skill, must be developed through practice. A distracted runner is an easy target. You better believe it!

Be aware of blind spots coming up? Corners cover with large trees. Has that car already passed you? Strange looking people that you have never seen before at the park where you usually run. What are those two guys doing on your path? Are they running? Are they looking around like if they were lost?

Why you are closing in to them if they are running too? Keep all this in your head when you are running and you won't go wrong.

Flexibility

If you think something is wrong, **Alter** your route, cross the street. Don't fell cowardly or stupid. Or you prefer to be mugged or assault?

Tips

It's crucial to your safety to stay perceptive. Remember the fundamental instructions:

1. Motion.   3-Run, hide, escape
2. Noise.   4-Fight

SELF-DEFENSE DEFINITION

Deadly force means when a person believes that he/she thinks needs to take action necessary for the defense of oneself or others against an attack. A person must only use the force necessary to deal with the circumstances.

Verbal Commands: The skill to speak effectively is essential. Reply to people; do not react. When you react it indicates that you're being manipulated. When you are responding, you are in control.

Actions that may cause death or bodily harm to the criminal is justified in self-defense, only in circumstances where a person believes that such action is necessary to prevent you or others from being killed or badly hurt.

Self-Defense Means

Is the action a person may take to protect himself from an attack from a criminal or criminals by countering attack.

In the United States, you are allowed to use lethal force to protect yourself and others.

Is your right to use deadly force to prevent physical injury, deadly force can be used only if you fear serious physical injury or death

So here you have it. Somewhere else in this book I advise you to find out and read to familiarize yourself with the state laws in self-defense in your state. I think it's necessary for anybody today, at least to have an idea of these laws.

You don't have to become an expert, just read them over and learn some about them

Stand your ground, Duty to Retreat and Castle Doctrine

Florida made history in 2005 when it passed the first "Stand Your Ground" law in the United States. Many states have enacted "Stand your Ground" laws; you should check the state you live in.

State self-defense laws fall into one of three categories:

Stand your Ground, Duty to Retreat and Castle Doctrine.

Stand your ground:

This law allows anyone in an imminent danger of death or bodily harm to fight back with deadly force. The person in danger has no duty to retreat when faced with a violent or threatening situation and can respond with force right away, without first make an effort to back away.

Duty-to-retreat:

This law requires individuals to retreat from threatening situations and only use deadly force as the last option.

Castle Doctrine:

Deadly force can only be used on their own property such as own home, yard, office. This is called **"castle exception"** from the expression **"A man's home is his castle".** There is no duty to retreat.

At the time of writing according to the **National Conference on State Legislatures**, a person has no duty to retreat if they are attacked in a place where they are legally permitted to be. These include

Alabama	Idaho	Michigan
Alaska	Indiana	Mississippi
Arizona	Kansas	Missouri
Florida	Kentucky	Montana
Georgia	Louisiana	Nevada

Murder begins where self-defense ends.
Georg Buchner.

Preventing Strategies

Awareness and **prevention** strategies must become habits and automatic. Keep an eye on people watching or following you, ambush places, and escape routes. Think once in a while which route you would take, which corner would you turn, where you would stop, if someone is following you.

If you are in the mall, where would you go? Just practice in your mind once in a while all kinds of scenarios and your actions. This simple exercise will wake your mind. Like a game you will become better if you play this kind of game in your mind once in a while.

You must be able to recognize a dangerous person or situation. This will make you safer.

 A real self-defense accomplishment is when nothing happens!

If you realize the problem **soon** the more options you have to resolve it.

You are less likely to be selected as a **target** if you follow the steps above.

Attitude is a little thing that makes a big difference.
Winston Churchill

Keep up with the news

Listen to the news to learn criminal patterns and factors that ends in violent crimes. What is in the news in your city? How burglaries, muggings, or rapes, are being executed in your town or city. How? Where? Keep this fresh in your mind.

Learn from this information. So when you are in a similar position you remember the news and become aware that you are placing yourself in a bad situation. Without awareness, you become an easy target for a criminal.

Avoidance is always the best self-defense strategy. The first line of defense against a violent situation is to **avoid it**.

Trust **your instinct** and **do not hesitate**. The more aware you are, the more you will prevent an attack.

You must keep an eye on:

Your environment	Your intuition	Crime tactics in your area

While doing your daily activities, walking, driving, and shopping.

Look out for:
People around you
Places where people can hide and surprise you
Location you are traveling from and to.
Location you are going to drive thru
Where are you going to walk from and to
Where are you going to park?
The time you are going to get out of work, the mall or the movie theater.

"Nothing in the world is more dangerous than sincere ignorance and conscientious stupidity."

Martin Luther King Jr.

Preoccupied

The **perfect** moment the criminal is looking and waiting for is when you are preoccupied, worried, tired, or sleeping, because this is the moment for him to attack you because you will be easily surprised. Muggings and pickpockets are crimes of opportunity. If you are with your hands occupied, talking on the phone, carrying groceries, setting young kids into the car, you look like an essay victim to a felon.

Become an intelligent, very **hard target** and the criminal will pass you for another easy target.

You must do

Appear very confident
Must be alert
Look at them in the eyes
Confront orally if you must
Resist as much as you can or decide to run.

Project Confidently

Walk with an upright stature, Keep your head up and **look** straight ahead.

Do not look down.

Don't be looking back every few minutes. You must **look** back once in a while, but don't overdo it. It may look like a sign of insecurity to the criminal.

In the eyes

Look at them square in the **eye**. Then, you can look somewhere else, but you must look at them in the eyes and return your eyes at them, repeat these movements with your eyes.

Facing the moment

No matter what you do, you may have to **face** a criminal one day. Think what you would do if that ever happens to you. How would you react? Would you fight, run, what?

Try not to show you are **scared**. We all are in a situation like that, don't let anybody fools you and tell you otherwise. Make **eye** contact and speak with a **loud,** clear voice. Do not **negotiate**. Do not allow the attacker to make decisions for you because any power you give up will automatically become his.

If he asks you for your wallet or watch give it to him with strength and integrity. You also need to think before this ever-happens to you, what you will fight for. It's never a good tactic to **fight** unless you are going to get **hurt**. Try to figure out fast what your attacker wants. You want to **get out** of the situation as **fast** and safely as possible. Do not assume is just a mugging, or that he is alone and that he is not going to hurt you. Don't **assume anything** until the situation is over and you are far away from the predator or criminal. It is a good idea to be abrupt and even rude. To send him a message that you are going to cooperate, but to a point. You also need to use your **common sense**.

Sometimes the situation starts without **you realizing it**. For example, someone might offer to walk or run with you. Or ask you if you need any help loading your gear in your car. Said, **"No"**, you do not need to justify it to anyone. Said **No** in a loud and clear voice, do not say anything else. Don't worry thinking you came out rude. Better be rude than sorry. If someone demands your wallet throw it to the ground far away from you and run the other way. If he is after your wallet he will run to pick it up and run out of there. If he runs after you and forget about the wallet. It's clear to you now that you are dealing with a physical assault and can prepare for it.

Courage is grace under pressure.
Ernest Hemingway

165

Getting help

Getting help is not a simple matter. Most people will not get involved in these types of situations. Since they know they will probably have to testify if the crook gets arrested. Or they think is probably a love scene. Tell them "This **stranger** is after me" Ask them "Call the police now" or" Please stand next to me" if you approach someone like this, they probably will help you.

Physical attacks
If you have been attacked you need to use as much force you can use. No way out, defend yourself with all you got. It's now or never. Don't worry about hurting your attacker because he is going to hurt you bad if he has the opportunities. So fight hard and fight nasty.

The attacker is violating your personal space and making you retreat. He tries to back you into a wall or corner if he can. **Don't let him.**

Hold your ground, move slightly to the side if you can. Don't take your eyes from the attackers. If you do, you are going to be distracted for a few seconds and he is going to land the first blow.

In another part of this book I told you that balance is the most important aspect in a fight, not speed or power. No self-defense technique is effective if you are off balance. If you lose your balance you are going to go to the ground and in the ground you are 99% in the attacker's hands. So, avoid being thrown to the ground like if your life depends on it, it does.

As much as 95% of attacks start with a grab or a punch. If someone grabs your wrist or shoulder remember that the rest of your body is still completely free.

You can kick, push, punch, use your elbow, slap, bite, head butt, or even use your voice. Targets like the eyes, knees and throat are not well protected by muscle and no matter how big or strong these parts are very vulnerable in everybody, even the big and strong criminals.

When somebody challenges you, fight back. Be brutal, be tough.
Donald Trump

166

Weapons

Feel free to use any weapons at your disposal. Keys, sticks, bottles, pen, pencils, umbrellas or anything else at hand can be a big advantage. Carrying a weapon like pepper spray or mace is a personal decision. Be careful with weapons like that can be taken away from you. Sometimes remember that they might not work. So it's up to you if you want or decide to use or carried one of these weapons personally don't trust them too much.

If your attacker has a weapon, you need to be very careful. Very careful!

Personal weapons

Stun guns and Tasers

Stun guns use high voltage and low amperage to temporarily disable an attacker for several minutes. The stun gun also interrupts voluntary muscle movement. Each state has its own laws and regulations. Stun guns are battery-powered devices designed to deliver an electric shock to an attacker.

Stun guns can't be fired from a distance, but still, stun guns are some of the most effective defenses you can carry without using lethal force. Stun gun needs to touch the skin when you discharged to be effective.

Tasers (also battery-powered) a Taser can be propelled up to 15 feet away, most fire two steels dart attached secure by wires back to the piece, and both dart has to pierce into the skin to be successful. As long as the dart is connected to the skin you can continue shocking the attacker.

Often the criminal can wreck the wires, even if the aggressor fall when he gets hit with one, yet he can attack you in no time.

They are supposed to inflict pain, fatigue of their muscles, and disrupting voluntary muscle control.

Stun guns and Tasers are legal depending where you live. Many states restrict the ownership or use of stun guns or Tasers by people other than the police.

These are some of the States where Stun Guns are restricted. Check your State if you are planning to buy one.

Hawaii
Massachusetts
Michigan
New Jersey
New York
Rhode Island
Wisconsin

You should check with a lawyer or your police department.

Do they work?

In reality, sometimes these devices fall short of getting the job done.

The downside of this device to be effective, the stun gun, must be held in contact with the criminal body, for an x-number of seconds. Even the new ones coming out still have the original problem; you must hold the device against the thug for various seconds.

If you are planning to buy one of these, try to buy the new one more powerful, the older model, used to have an output a range of five to 14 watts.

The new ones have an output of 18 to 26 watts, much better and more powerful.

The truth of the matter is the efficacy of these devices, depends on the wattage, contact time with the aggressor, battery strength. With the Taser you have to aim and hit the target. Sometime very hard to do under the stress and the commotion movement of an attack taking place. Not easy to accomplish, plus you only have at the most two darts.

Key chains

There are many different kinds of chili peppers ranging from Jalapenos, Chilepin, and Cayenne. They all have one thing in common. They all contain a substance that is very powerful alkaloid called capsaicin (cap-say-a-sin). You can get them is key chain, spray cans, etc.

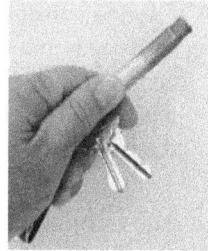

Spray rings

Pepper Spray self-defense ring with replaceable pepper spray canisters empowers a woman or man while jogging, dating, working or anywhere against attack, rape, violence or crisis. Some people think is great, others disagree, they claim that is too small of a spray. Pepper sprays are great options when it is illegal or uncomfortable to carry a firearm.

OC paper Spray

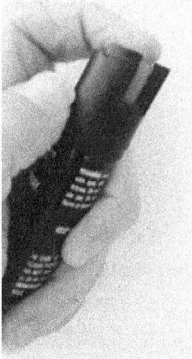

Pepper sprays are a very protective tool, particularly popular with teenage girls and woman who don't feel good owning or carrying a gun. The most popular and effective defensive spray is OC (Oleoresin Capsicum), what people call pepper spray. Pepper spray is derived from hot peppers. When it gets into the eyes is very painful. Causes hampered vision or maybe temporary blindness. If a small amount is inhaled, it constricts the bronchial tubes, making the attacker choke and cough. Today there are a number of quality pepper sprays on the market.

The Peeper Blaster-effective to approximately 13 feet, and a high –speed of 90 mph. The great point is that the assailant does not have to be really close to you.

The police and federal law enforcement has used them for decades. It is very good for a self-defense tool. In fact, don't expect someone to fall and surrender when sprayed. I personally have doubts that the spray may not work with some violent, people. I have seen people been sprayed in the face and still charging and reaching the person who defended himself with such a spray and still being able to beat the person who used the spray on them.

The information presented is not in any form legal advice. You must check with your local authorities to obtain your state or city regulations. Keep in mind that Federal law prohibits the carrying of any type of chemical weapon on commercial aircraft, courts, in federal buildings, and prisons.

Alarms and whistles

A personal alarm is a noisemaker, something that makes a loud, piercing noise when it is set off. Powered whistles by lungs are often referred as "rape whistles". Do they work? Not really. Don't let the sales person tells you otherwise. Don't believe that someone will come to help you when you blow a whistle or set off a siren, they won't. Don't fall for it. It is going to take you a couple of seconds to do it. Seconds that the attacker is not going to waste.

The Flashlight for Self-Defense

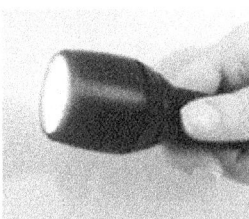

They are legal to carry in every state in the U.S, Flashlights are Discreet. High-lumen tactical flashlights can be taken into places like a movie theaters or airplanes where guns are banned. Shine it directly into the thug eyes, for three to four seconds, he is going to be disorientated and semi-blindness. After disoriented him, strike his face with the flashlight as hard as you can. That gives you time to either flee or attack.

To be effective for self-defense, it needs to be at least 120 Lumens of light output. Your flashlight should be no bigger than the size of your palm.

THE LASER FLASLIGHT

Personal protection that temporarily disorients an attacker, potentially stopping a rape or an assault before it happens. You can carry it everywhere; maintain your distance and blinding a potential attacker or attackers, giving you enough time for you to escape.

If you shine a laser flashlight to a criminal eyes, instantly will disorientate the attacker and blind him, allowing your escape. A powerful green laser will burn the retinas, and possibly lasting damage to the eyes. The only time for shining a laser in somebody's eyes is if that person is attempting to kill you or do you severe harm. If you react fast you will shock your opponent affecting their ability to attack you, giving you time to run or escape. Laser light disorientation is powerful.

A Laser flashlight to function as a self-defense needs to be:

Pocket-sized to easily carry
Simple to switch on
Strongly bright
Dependable
Compact

Screaming is much better and effective; a voice has an impact that cannot be compared to a mechanical sound. Combine screaming with running away, kicking, striking effective blows.

"Use only that which works, and take it from any place you can find it."

Bruce Lee (Tao of Jeet Kune Do)

STREET SMARTS

1- Study a map before going out if you are in an unknown place, once on the street avoids looking like a tourist.

2- Dress down. Don't use your best cloth or jacket; this is a sign for the predator.

3- Avoid jewelry; even if they are fake, consider not wearing a wedding ring if you are in unfamiliar places.

4- Use a money belt around your waist under your clothes.

5- Beware getting off a bus or train; riding stairs and escalators, these are favorite places to be mugged.

6- Carry just one credit card and photocopies of important documents.

7- Divide money for small and larger purchases so you don't have to expose a wallet or purse full of bills.

8- Become familiar with foreign currency before you use it.

9- Have gratuities ready, so you don't have to be opening your wallet or purse.

10- If a car starts to follow you, turn and walk the opposite way.

11- Ask for directions only to families or women with children.

12- When walking on sidewalks, keep your handbag away from the street side, this way it's much harder for a thieve to steal it and run across the street.

13- When you are using escalators, stay away from the opposite ramp. Think about it, it is much safer this way.

Ask for directions to only families or women with children.

172

Traveling Smart

1-Write your work address in luggage tags instead of your home address.

2-Ask flight attendants on the plane about the safety of your destination before you actually arrive.

3-Always place your belongings on your car seat right away then get in the car

4-Make sure you've arrived at your destination before getting out of a taxi. Pay while still in the car; make sure you've gotten the proper change.

5-Stay close and keeps an eye to your belonging when passing through airport security. Never take your eyes from them.

6-Sitting in a restaurant or other public area, place your carry-on bag on the floor and place your foot through the strap; don't leave it loose. Same in the restroom. Very important, especially in a public restroom.

7-Bring your own mobile phone or rent one. Place the police # on speed dial. Very important.

8-If renting a car, park so you won't have to back out. It makes for a speedier escape.

GENERAL ADVICE

1-Must people only just check the weather of their destination; also learn when the **sun rises** and **sets**. This is a **must** if you are in an unfamiliar place.

2-Check onto the Internet and obtain **safety info** about a place you're planning to visit.

> ***Self-defense is not only our right; it is our duty.***
> ***Ronald Reagan***

173

Chapter 5-The Predator, Rapist

The attack

Violent crime data show the criminal sees a woman as weak and easy targets. Attacks on woman are usually made by men who are positive none expecting any kind of defense. Most of the woman has probably been harassed at some time.

Maybe at work, walking or by a phone call. Many sexual assaults believe it or not are committed by someone you know, a friend, the car mechanics, the grocery boy, or even the boyfriend or husband friend.

Many women's self-defense programs teach martial art's techniques that are complex and unrealistic to use effective by most average women. This is true.

Don't trust a clean cut, honest looking stranger. Thugs and criminals they do not look like monsters. They often look like a very nice guy.

Tactic

The attacker in some cases may try before to determine if you are an easy target too intimidated or if you are easily scare and find out your vulnerability. If you are firm, assertive and take a position of loudness. He is likely to go and look for another victim. Yell as loud as you can, 'stop, leave me alone'.

Rape

It is a real problem in the United States today. The United States has the highest rape percentage among countries which report such statistics. It is four times higher than that of Germany, 13 times higher than that of England and 20 times higher than that of Japan. The Justice Department says that 8 % of all-American women will be victims of rape or attempted rape in their lifetime.

Evaluate surrounding, a street corner, parking lot, elevator, public bathroom, etc. Consider if you have a way to escape. Back doors, walking away with three or four friends, is there a police officer closed by, a telephone.

Are doors, large trees, fences, walls, trash cans, shrubbery impeding you escape? Can you hide from your adversary at least temporarily? Can you use trees, the dark, big objects to hide and evade your attacker from getting to you?

Is he unaccompanied? Are there two or more? What are his intentions with you? How distant is he from you? Can you reach a lighted area or traffic street? Do you think he is drunk, high? Is he breathing hard? What is he saying? Does he carry a weapon? Pay attention to everything around you, these are important clues for you to respond in your best self-defense probable way.

The first action a woman should take is to look, by knowing if there is a dangerous situation you have the advantage for some precious seconds in which to decide your plan of action.

She may cross the street suddenly; walk in into a house even if it is a private house. Maybe open her purse and put her hand inside to make believe she is carrying a weapon.
On the other hand, if you don't look and an attacker gets you from behind, you are allowed to be placed in the worst situation.

Yell!

Yelling is a particular defense measure that every woman should know. How many times we heard in the news the neighbors were attracted by the screams.

In a parking lot

The same techniques in the section or parking apply to a woman in this section. I repeated them again here. Read them again; make a note in your head.

Park near lights, so you can see right away anyone standing near your car, so you can go back to get another person, call security or the police if necessary to walk you out

Don't park between vans or trucks because this is a great hiding spot for criminals.

Park in well-lighted areas, and close by to where you are going as possible.

I have seen people many times, specially woman when they get to their car, place the bags first in the trunk or other side of the car, then inside the car with the car still off, put on or changes their glasses, sometimes even looking into a storage bag to check something they just bought. Even talk on the phone still with the car off, finally they put on the seatbelt and then turn the car and leave, they took maybe four to eight minutes on this. More than enough for a predator or rapist to attack.

Don't do this ever, you are inviting trouble and I see it every day, next time you visit a mall, check what I just told you and see it yourself. This is what you should do.
Look at the big pictures as you walk to your car, is there anything strange happening, like a car on with a guy in it?

You should get in your car, lock the doors, start the engine , place the car in reverse, back up, place the car in forward and then put your Seatbelt, move forward, then put on your glasses, the radio, but this only took a couple of minutes.

If a rapist was going to go after you, your car is already moving forward with no obstacles in front of you like a parked car or a wall.

You are free to drive quickly if you notice something wrong.
If something makes you feel uneasy, get into the car quickly, lock the doors, and drive away.

The best protection any woman can have... is courage.
Elizabeth Cady Stanton

Date Rape Drugs

There are many several drugs that have been used in recent rapes. The " **Date Rape Drugs** " are the ones that single women need to be extra careful about, especially when traveling overseas.
The company that makes this drug has taken certain steps to prevent its misuse:

1. They have colored it blue
2. They say it will sparkle on contact with a liquid.
3. They say it will float at the top of a drink for about 20
   minutes after having been placed in the liquid.

Finding proof that "Date Rape Drugs" were used is extremely complicated to obtain, as traces of the drugs do not linger in the body for a long period.

Of course, many other drugs have been used in date rapes; including Methadone, LSD and Ecstasy to mention a few.

Some tips on how to avoid falling victim to date rape drugs are:

A-Don't ever leave your drinks unattended.

B- Always watch as your drink is being served!

C-If you feel sick or dizzy, call a friend over the phone or ask for the manager of the establishment, don't waste time. If you call the manager, tell him you are feeling sick or dizzy and ask him to call a taxi to take you home or to your hotel right away. This way you know you are getting into a real taxi, and by involving him you have a reputable person knowing about the situation.

D- Keep in mind that alcohol or drugs will reduce your ability to be in control.

This is a precaution you need to take, no matter if you are in your home country and especially abroad when traveling. Don't trust anyone.

If something makes you feel uneasy leave right away

Rohypnol- "The Date Rape Drug of Choice"

The three most common date rape drugs are:

Rohypnol. Rohypnol is also known by more names.
Example:

Ruffies
Mexican Valium
Poor Man's Quaalude

Ketamine also known by more names. Here are a few:
Black Hole
Bump
Super Acid

GHB/GBL also known by other names. Here are a few:
Rufies
Liquid E
Fantasy
What do the drugs look like?

- **Rohypnol** is a pill that dissolves in liquids. Some are small, round, and white. Newer pills are oval and green-gray in color. Once slipped into a drink, a dye in these new pills makes clear liquids turn bright blue and makes dark liquids turn cloudy. The color changes might be hard to see in a dark drink, like cola or dark beer, or in a dark room, the pills with no dye are still available. The pills may be ground up into a powder.

- **GHB and GBL** has a few forms: a liquid with no odor or color, white powder, and pill. It might give your drink a slightly salty taste.

- **Ketamine** comes as a liquid and a white powder.

This answer is based on source information from the National Women's Health Information Center.

Department of Justice data-2018

The study replicates findings in a number of other studies, which tend to find that close to one in five women in college are sexual-assault victims.

Sexual violence on campus is pervasive.

11.2% of all students experience rape or sexual assault through physical force, violence, (among all graduate and undergraduate students).

Information:
https://www.campussafetymagazine.com/safety/sexual-assault-statistics

http://www.newsweek.com/during-freshman-year-186-female-students-may-experience

Us Department of justice statics 2017

Approximately 20 million out of 112 million women (18.0%) in the United States has been raped during their lifetime.

Bureau of Justice Statistic's National Criminal Victimization Survey:

- In 2016, U.S. residents age 12 or older experienced 5.7 million violent victimization's—a rate of 21.1 victimization's per 1,000 peoples age 12 or older.
- The rate of stranger violence (8.2 per 1,000 people) was higher than the rate of intimate partner violence (2.2 per 1,000).
- In 2016, U.S. households experienced 15.9 million property crimes—a rate of 119.4 per 1,000 households.

- Motor vehicle thefts (80%) were the most likely of all crime types to be reported to police.

In 2016, a total of 1.3% of all people age 12 or older experienced one or more violent victimization's.

College rape

- In 2013, females ages 18 to 24 had the highest rate of rape and sexual assault victimization compared to females in all other age groups. Within the 18 to 24 age groups, victims could be identified as students enrolled in a college, university, trade school or vocational school or as non-students. Among student victims, 20% of rape and sexual assault victimizations were reported to police, compared to 32% reported among non-student.
- The rate of rape and sexual assault was 1.2 times higher for non-students (7.6 per 1,000) than for students (6.1 per 1,000). For both college students and non-students, the offender was known to the victim in about 80% of rape and sexual assault victimizations. Most (51%) student rape and sexual assault victimization's occurred while the victim was pursuing leisure activities away from home.
  Information:
  https://www.rainn.org/statistics/campus-sexual-violence

Don't be statics

Sexual Violence May Occur at a Higher Rate at Certain Times of the Year

More than 50% of college sexual assaults occur in either, August, September, October, or November.

Students are at an increased risk during the first few months of their first and second semesters in college.

Between 20% and 25% of women will experience a completed and/or attempted

80% of sexual assault and rape victims are under the age of 30

44% of sexual assault and rape victims are under the age of 18

Students living in sorority houses and on-campus dormitories are three times and 1.4 times (respectively) more likely to be raped than students living off-campus.

38% of college-aged women who have been sexually victimized while in college had first been victims prior to entering college, making past victimization the best predictor of future victimization.

At least 50% of college student sexual assaults are associated with alcohol. During their freshman year of college, 15 % of women are raped while incapacitated from alcohol or drugs.

Information: https://www.usnews.com/news/

Preventing Rape

Experts agree that rape is more than just a sex offense. They say that it's an act of violence against another person.

For example, according to the U.S. Department of Justice in 2017, more than 20 million **female rapes/sexual** assaults out of 1120 million women (18.0%) in the United States has been raped during their lifetime.

According to the Bureau of Justice Statistics, the most in danger at risk groups are **young**, unmarried women between the ages of **16** and **19** who come from a low-income home. The second most at risk group was in the **20** to **24** age's group; and the third most vulnerable group was **12** to **15** years of age. Statistics also show that a woman's chance of being raped are about twice as high if she is black.

In the majority of reported cases, the rapist **knew the victim** before the rape attack. In fact, 74.2 percent of all rape/sexual assaults involved a non-stranger, with 47 percent of imprisoned rapists declaring that they **knew** their victim(s) before raping them.

On the victim side, 33 percent of female rape victims, ages **18** and older, said that they didn't know their attacker. Or, putting it another way, 67 percent of these **rape victims** said that they either knew or were acquainted with their attacker.

What to Do?

Most people feel secure behind the locked doors of their own homes. Statistics show that **37.4 percent** of female rapes took place occurred **inside** the victim's home.

This means that in many cases, these victims opened their door to someone they trusted to be a friend or an **acquaintance**.

This is why, unless you are very familiar with the person calling outside your door you should never allow them to enter. Of course, not all rapes are perpetrated by someone the victim knows. In many cases, the rapist is a stranger to the victim.

Approximately one in five (18.3 percent) woman and one in 71 men (1.4 percent) voiced rape at some point in their lives.

One in 20 women suffered sexual violence other than rape.

44 percent of female rape victims were raped before the age 18.

About 29.9 percent of female victims were first raped between the age of 18 and 24.

Stay with people, go to people, and stay where others can see you. The rapist worst fear is the fear of getting caught, so you should drop to the ground if you need to in order to prevent him from carrying you away if he is trying to take you by force to another location, but only do this if you can't run.

Attract attention

There are some issues you should think before fighting back, according to the FBI, such as the location of confrontation, type of victim and motivation of the attack.

The rapist will tell you "don't scream or I'll kill you." He's telling you exactly what will spoil his plan. Ruin his plan, create a disturbance, scream, throw things, and blow the horn. If you think you should yell "fire" go right ahead, do it, spoil his plan right there and there is a 99 percent chance he will run away.

It is a must that all women should always **know** their caller before they **open** the door. If the caller tells you that he has a genuine business inside your home or apartment, you should closely examine his credentials and personal identification.

This should be done through-the **door peep-hole** lens or an **intercom system**. A combine intercom/camera system should be installed because this will allow you not only to talk to the callers but to see who they are as well. This will help women; make sure they know **who** the caller is before **opening** the door.

Here's a list of do and donts a woman alone must do to prevent a rapist from taking advantage of them:

- Use only your **first initial** and **last name** when marking your mailbox.

- Use only your **first initial** and **last name** in a telephone book listing.

- Use only the **best** locks obtainable, and be sure to have a **deadbolt** lock installed on all of your doors.

- Install a good quality lock on your bedroom door.

- Install a **telephone** in the bedroom. If possible, buy a telephone with a speed-dial key on it so you can program one of them to dial "**911**."

- Because some crook will first cut the phone lines before they attempt to make contact with their would-be victim keep a charged cell phone next to your bed.

- If you're still unsure of the caller after checking their identification, call the company or utility they say they work for and ask for that person's supervisor.

- Show no signs of predictability by leaving **certain lights** on in your home no matter whether you're at home or away. This will keep a would-be criminal **guessing**.

- Have an **answering** machine to screen your phone calls so a rapist or any other criminal cannot **use it** to see if you are home.

Intelligence is the ability to adapt to change.
Stephen Hawking

Rape

Nearly more than 50 % of all rapes occur in the victims own bedrooms.

These predators look for the weak, shy or disoriented victim. The one that seems not have been aware of her surroundings. The knife's is the weapon rapist prefer to use. Never underestimate the danger of a knife. According to experts, there are three kinds of rapist.

Power Rapist
1-Wants his victim to enjoy the rape
2-Wants verbal support
3-Most of the time he is well educated.

Anger Rapist
1-Angry, hateful
2-Blames his troubles on woman
3-Use vulgarity
4-Very dangerous, use alcohol or drugs when the attack is taking place.

Sadist Rapist
1-The most dangerous of rapist
2-Employs torment and cruelty
3-Will kill the victim most of the time
4- Extremely dangerous. The victim must fight from the beginning of the situation for her life.

Never ever try to De–escalate a sexual assault or rape. This obedience could further stimulate the rapist.
There are plenty of proofs that reveal that a woman is less likely to be raped if she fights back. Of course self –defense action is not for everybody.

You have to think the predator is out there watching you and planning his move. His best ability is to surprise you, also to pick ambush zones where he can attack you. The ambush he looks for could be corners, behind ambushes, between cars, the elevator, building stairs.

Rape

Every two minutes a woman is raped.

Every day four women are killed during a rape.

75% of rape is committed by a man the victim knows.

25% of rape takes place in a public place.

Knives are the most frequently use weapon among rapist.

Criminals like knives because-They are silent-easier to conceal

If you should ever be in a threatening situation
A-Do whatever it takes to get away.
B-Plan ahead what you would do if you were threatened.

Rape is a very serious crime and is classified along with murder.

1-There are serious consequences such as pregnancy, AIDS, herpes and other Venereal diseases.

2-There are also serious psychological effects that can be permanently damaging.

1. The median age for female molestation victims under 18 is 9.6 years old.
2. There are new, 400,000 victims of sexual assault every year.
3. There are over 550,000 registered sex offenders in the US.
4. There are over 100,000 sex offenders that fail to register in the US.
5. 76% of serial rapists claim they were molested as children.
6. Over 40% of male juvenile delinquents were molested as children

You Don't Have To Be A Victim!

What to do if you believe you have been drugged and raped

First thing to do is to Call 911 or have a true friend take you to a hospital emergency room. Don't urinate, douche, shower, rinse your hands, change clothes, or eat or drink before you go. These possibly will be rape evidence.

Once in the hospital call and tell the police exactly what you remember. Be straightforward, nothing you did counting drinking alcohol or doing drugs can defend or authorize rape.

Ask the hospital to give you a urine (pee) test that can be used to test for day rape drugs. These kinds of drugs leave your system quickly. Rohypnol stays in the body for a few hours; Rohypnol can be detected in the urine up to 72 hours after taking it. GHB leaves the body in 12 hours. Don't urinate before going to the hospital.

Don't clean where the assault might have occurred. Possibly there will be evidence left behind, such as in a drinking glass or bed sheets.

Get treatment from a counseling and treatment center as soon as you can. Shame, self-reproach, fear, is a normal feeling. A counselor will be able to help you work through the healing process. Making a call to a crisis center or a hot-line is a good place to start. One national hotline is the national sexual assault hot-line at 1-800-656-HOPE.

If something makes you feel uneasy leave right away

Sex attacks

Sexually remarks, Jeers, groping, flashing, assault, street harassment it is a form of gender violence and it's a human right violation. A large number of women will face gender-based street harassment by strangers in their life. It is a common misjudging that criminals are stupid. On the contrary, some are precisely observers, evaluating your walk, talk and others indicator. They are careful predators; they know what they need to look for.

Ambush zones

These are strategic locations from which criminals launch their attacks. These zones are everywhere; these places could be, behind three, corners, tables, cars, or in dark poorly lit area, Sex attacks are common when you are moving from one place to another. Many times happen when you go from your car to work or work to your home, walking to the parking lot, taking out the trash, or jogging down the road.

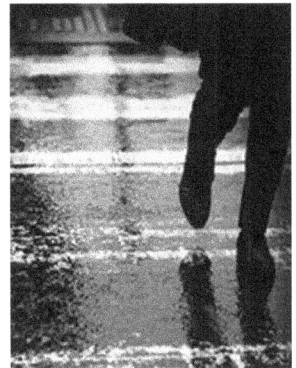

Your car key must be out of your pocket or purse and in your hand as you go from your office to your car. Don't fumble for your keys taking your concentration away from what is going on, around you. The keys can be used as a weapon to strike into the eyes or face if attacked since you already have a weapon in your hand.

Run away from your assailant if possible depending how close you are to a safe place, your shoes, your clothing, your physical condition, etc.

If you must, throw bags or anything in the attacker's face, yell loud, very loud as you run away. Yell for help "Help! Call the Police". Fire! Call attention, make noises the louder the better.

Red flags for a woman when arriving home

A neighbor that you almost don't know, tells you, let me help you with those bags of groceries. Let me help you get them inside.

He may tell you, I'm going to your floor anyway. Or he may tell you an insult to get you to talk to someone you otherwise wouldn't.

Maybe he tells you, you can leave the door open, I'll leave as soon as I put the bags down, I promise.

These are all red-flags-pay attention.

Consent situations

Be up-front with a new date communicate clearly your limits.

If your date touches in a sexual way, and he or she does not have your consent it is sexual assault. Tell him/ her right away. Tell a friend or family member where you are planning to go to and when you expect to get home at least in the beginning.

The most common mistakes women make that place them in a dangerous situation for getting kidnapped, attacked, and/or raped:

1. **When he pulls** a gun and orders you to get into his vehicle, getting into the attacker's car. He doesn't want to shoot you ...he wants you to get into the car so he or they can drive you to a deserted place and rape you. The police call such places "secondary crime scenes." Don't do it. Run screaming. I'll bet you he will just move on to an easier target.

2. **A man drives alongside** of you pointing at your car pretending something is wrong and you pull over. If this happens, don't stop, Never pull over, drive to the nearest populated gas station and look the car over yourself. Do not accept a stranger help. Many women have fallen for this trick.

3. **Keeping doors unlock** while driving. I have read several cases where the attacker just simply walks up to a woman's car while she's at a traffic light and jumps in with his gun or knife drawn. Don't allow this to happen to you.

4. **Opening the main front** door when you have not identified who is there. I've heard countless cases where the attacker gains access to its victims simply by knocking on their door, just like that. No noise, no confrontation, just that simple. Don't let an attacker get into your home this way. He then has all the time he wants and a private, soundproof place to attack you.

5. **Not paying attention** enough in a parking lot. Too many women are abducted from parking lots or even raped in the parking lot. Always look in your back seat before entering your car. Look for attackers both inside and in between parking cars. Always look around and behind you when are walking to your car. You may appear paranoid and funny to others, but an attacker will think twice about approaching someone who appears so aware of what's going on.

6. **Most women trust a clean cut**, honest looking stranger. Predators and rapist often look like they could be your friendly grocer, bank teller, waiter, neighbor, etc.

"Criminals seek those unaware"

Notes for woman

A. Easy target

A mugger looks for a woman who appears unguarded. Talking on your cell, or texting a message makes you an excellent target for a crook.

B. Careful after-hours

Visit the ATM early in the day, if possible in a crowded area. Don't walk home at night by yourself; don't take the subway alone after hours. Don't wait for the bus by yourself in a lonely dark corner. Keep your eyes open to your surroundings. Predators are always in the lookout for opportunities.

C. Be alert

Parking lot, stairwells, and pathways, are places for easy attacks. You're distracted, and your hands are carrying packages, and sometimes the parking lot is lonely and dark.

D. Your purse

If the robber wants your purse, throw your purse as far as you can, and run toward the light, people or in the direction of a store.

E. Strollers and babies

You must be really careful, where you park, how far from the store, how dark. When you leave the store you are going to be extremely occupied, with your stroller, loading it into your car, loading the Baby, and the packages. If you are not careful you can become an easy target for a thug. Again, awareness is the key.

F. Physically attacks

This changes your perspective completely, you must defend yourself at any cost, defend yourself anyway you can with anything you carry on at that moment, an umbrella, keys, pen, cane, or even perfume spray. Remember to keep yelling constantly. The noise and the commotion will make the attacker leave as quickly as he can.

Tactics:

Don't take the same trail or street every day, change your route, don't walk or run in the same direction or at the same time.

Jog with a friend or friends better yet.

Trust your instincts, if you feel uncomfortable, get out of there right away and fast.

Don't talk to strangers. A must, no matter how friendly he seems. Let friends know where you are going, route and when you are expected back.

Stay on the trail. Don't go in the bushes or away from the trail for no reason whatsoever. Stay on course. See anything suspicious, take action right away, don't delay your action, go back, move direction, get on the phone. Take action **now**.

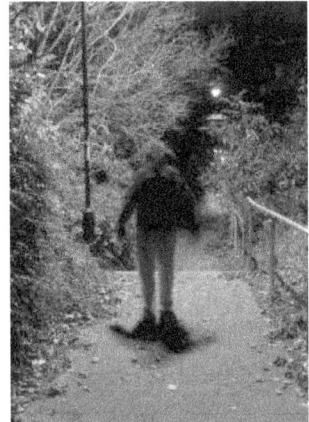

Don't jog or walk in an **isolated area**, pick one with people traffic.

Your mind-set is your primary weapon
Jeff Cooper

Ladies walking or jogging

Forget what people or your self-defense teacher tells you. A woman is no match for a man, especially if this male is intoxicated in some drug. That's it.

If a stranger approaches you, don't talk, if you have to talk, tell him you are not alone, say your friends are just behind or ahead of you, or waiting for company any time by now.

Sometime a cell phone does not work in the woods. Try your phone in the area you run or walk to find out if you have reception and where there is not.

Always be alert of your surroundings

Have you considered carrying **Pepper Spray** for Self Defense? Maybe is a good idea.

1-While you yell stop, bring the spray up, aim and shoot.
2-Run away fast, and call 911!

Distrust and caution are the parents of security
Benjamin Franklin

Tips for Woman Defense

Let me give you an example of a woman I know, let's call her Vicky, Vicky got to her second floor apartment pass 1:00 am one night, when she reaches her door and she was going to introduce her apt key, she realizes and she didn't know where this man came from, he was just behind her a foot or two away , already untying his pants, if she had opened her door he probably would have pushed her in, raped her, rob and probably hurt her bad or even kill her.

No, what she did, surprise the rapist that was spec ting a victim, she turn arounds and staring hitting him all over at the same time she was yelling with all her power , Police!, police! , fire, she kept yelling and hitting him all over his body, moving as much as she could and ripping his shirts.

In shock, surprise and scare off all the noise and commotion at that time of the night , knowing the next door neighbors were going to call the police he fleet running , while Vicky still follows him about 10 feet yelling , cursing and hitting him in the back,. She refuses to be a victim, what a scare that rapist Got! See the difference. The rapist and all of them want a victim, not a chance of getting arrested.

I'm going to call Anna the next case I know, unfortunately this lady got raped and hurt for life. This is her case. She came out of the store and got in her car without looking behind the front seat. A man pulls a knife in her neck from behind and asks her to drive to a lonely and dark spot where he raped her, rob her money and took her car.

This is was not the end of it, because he took all of her information and wallet, about a month later he try to get inside her house by force in the middle of the night, the noise woke her up, her sister and her mother, and it seems he was high on something because as she was calling the police the mother and sister were trying to prevent him from getting into the house by force, fighting with them.

When the police arrive and arrested him, he was still trying to force his way in by the window and forcefully with the mother and sister. Unfortunately, there were actions she could have taken to prevent being the victim or rape.

She should have looked inside her car before she got into, then she could have run away from the car yelling, making a big commotion back to the store, with probably ten or fifteen witness, the rapist would have run ,not after her, but away from her.

Another action she could have taken was step on the gas and hit a car from behind at a traffic light in a busy interception she passed, or place the car in reverse and hit the car behind her; also she could have thrown away the car keys in an interception. Or force her car into coming traffic and hit a car, anything to call attention to her right there and then.

All of this action should have been better than to drive to a dark, solitary place, to being raped like she was, she was lucky he did not kill her. If she had followed the steps above mention the rapist only chance of not getting caught was to run away and hide. He was not going to kill her in front of all those witness, no way.

If someone is in the car with a gun to your head run the engine and speed into anything, smashing the car. Your Air-Bag will save you. If the individual is in the rear seat he will get the worst of it.

Countless times you can see a victim being caught by the store camera in the evening news force to walk with the rapist right from the front of the store to be raped and kill later. The police call such places "secondary crime scenes." If a hoodlum takes you to a secondary crime scene there is a 99% possibility that you are not coming back alive, however, if you fight back you have a 99% chance of surviving.

No, the answer is to **fight right there**, **yell**, **scream, kick,** he is saying that he would kill you right there, placing fear into you and just intimidation you, if he takes you for sure he is going to kill you after he abuses you and do many bad things to you. **Fight;** with many people in front probably someone will come to your rescue, the security or even the police.

Never under any circumstances, **go with him**; take your **chance right** there in **front of everybody.** I'll bet you anything he will escape and go away to look for an easy prey or victim. Never leave the scene ever. Your chances are 99% higher to be killed, seriously injured or raped if you go with the criminal than if you run away right there (even if he promises not to hurt you).

Run away, yell for help, throw a rock through a store or car window, do whatever you can to attract attention. Make a scene, believe it; he is not going to stay around, if you react the way I recommend to.

Now if he wants your purse, jewelry, money or your car key, that's another story, give him anything he wants, but I **repeat**, **never eve**r go with him under any circumstances.

So the most important advice is **awareness**, fight, make noise and commotion right there, never, ever let him take you with him anywhere.

Take your chance's right where everybody can see you. Remember, though, to use the element of shock to your advantage. Keep your eyes open and don't give the rapist the opportunities to surprise you. They want victims, not a straggle in public with the chance of getting caught.

Abducted

Most kidnapping are carry out for sexual gratification, to satisfy their own personal satisfaction or to sell the girl/woman into a life of sex trafficking prostitution. Some could be for political agenda or for ransom if your family as money. In a circumstance like this, you must take action with a 100 % resistance, hesitation, almost certainly will get you abducted and killed.

You must fight back with all your strength to escape, by kicking, yelling, scratching, biting, pocking, forceful like an animal, the longer you fight, the more attention you are going to get, exactly what the abductor doesn't want. You turn out to be hard and difficult to handle, he will let you go and run off.

The chances of becoming a victim can be reduced if you increase your awareness of your surroundings.

Women's self-defense must contain the following advantages:

1. It had to be **useful** against any size attacker and stronger attacker.
2. It had to be **fast, effective** and **crucial!**
3. It had to contain a **minimum** amount, of **course of action**.

Predators will:

A- Select a target.

B- Tail you to identify practices and routes.

C- Select a site in her usual route; wait for her in the spot where he wants to abduct, rape, attack her, for many sexual predators, it possibly will be the back seat of his car.

You must notice if he is glancing through the magazine stand, and leaves the store at the identical time you leave.

Pay attention if you see him enter another store, you just entered.

Notice if he walks to the food court at the same time you do. Observe his demeanor: does he look anxious, watching you, wandering without a point.

Thugs, including rapists or sexual predators, study a target of opportunity.

Self-preservation tips for women returning to college campus

When new students arrive to the college grounds, many female undergrads will tour the new area, meet new friends, visit social events, maybe parties or get together in rooms dorm, or just walk to dorm at night from the library. Increased violence on campus is a reality, college students are at the highest risk of being sexually assaulted, frequently by someone they know.

Checkpoints ahead of time:

Exit door
A door with an exit sign over doesn't mean it's a safe exit; the door may lead to location dangerous for women. Exit doors that led to the outdoors ground level are best.

Improvised weapons
Everything can be modified into an impact weapon, a pen in your pocket, a ruler, your cell phone, your key. Always try to keep something handy that can be grabbed if confronted.

The purse
The purse can be used as a shield, hit the attacker's face or the groin.

Stop and pass
If you sense someone is following you, stop, allows that person to pass. Simulate you have to go in another route or presume to take a phone call, never expose your back to the person.
Don't be concerned, giving the impression as rude; go with your natural instinct. If something doesn't feel right to you, probably is.

If at any time a situation doesn't feel right, get out, and find a friend, even if you have to lie about it. Say you need to use the bathroom, or go outside, do whatever you need to do if you're feeling awkward or feeling the pressure. Your safety comes before someone else's feelings or what they may think of you.

Control your life.
Think before you share personal info. Posting social media updates on your activities or class schedules will allow someone to track your every move. You would never share personal information with a stranger, and then you shouldn't share it online.

People trust.
College environment creates a false feeling of security. Keep in mind that you just met these individuals; you may even feel like you have been best friends forever. Never assume that your new acquaintances will definitely be looking out for your best interests.

Stay alert.
Whether you are at a party or walking across campus, concentrate on what, is going around you. Try to take a well-trafficked route and avoid being isolated with someone that you don't know or trust. If your college grounds have a bus or public safety escorts that will walk you home at night, take advantage of them.

Make plans.
When going out, know beforehand who is going, and propose to stay together as a group. At all times have a designated sober friend in the group. Before you leave check that you have a fully charged phone, the number of a cab company, and cash to get you home. Maintain your phone on you at all times, in the event you find yourself in an unpleasant or dangerous situation.

Party smart.
Watch your drink at parties, this is a must. Don't accept a drink from individuals you don't trust or you don't know well. Only drink the one you got or prepared yourself. If you walk away from your drink, even for a couple of minutes, get a new one. Keep track of what you've drank, so that you can stay in control. If at any time you feel like you're getting sick or are too intoxicated, ask a friend or the

police officer to help you get to a safe place or to a hospital. Never ever allowed you to get into this circumstance.

Watch out for each other.
Stick all together in a group, particularly when going from one place to the next. If you are suspicious that an accompanying person has been drugged or needs medical attention because of over-intoxication or for any other reason, call 911.

Remember, you can always contact your resident assistant or campus police or call 911.

Safety is a cheap and effective insurance policy
Author Unknown

Sorority/Fraternity

Fraternities and sororities are social organizations at colleges and universities. They are prominent in the United States. When terms like 'sorority' or 'fraternity' comes to mind, it would mean colleges, universities, and having certain grouping, alliance, even having a special group.

Fraternity comes from a Latin word 'fraternus', which means brother. Is a group of men who are bound together because of a specific reason, friendship, brotherhood believing, a common goal or aspiration.

Differences between a fraternity and a sorority?
The fraternity has male members and sorority has female members. Some female groups call themselves fraternities, except that they put a special name.

Hazing

What is Hazing?
Some say it is a part of the initiation process, any activity expected of someone joining or participating in a group that humiliates, degrades, abuses, or endangers them regardless of a person's willingness to participate

Pledging for sororities and fraternities has always existed in college. No one knows how many students wake up after a night of pledging, with signs of physical and sexual abuse. This tradition is named hazing, a dangerous initiation procedure that has turned out to be common on college campuses, and for those who will do anything to be in that group.

Hazing usually includes:
Beating
Exceed drinking
Paddling
Spitting
Mental and physical intimidation

Safe Partying

Social activity gathering is part of university life on weekends, most students will experiment with partying.

Sexual assault is frequently at college parties. One in four women is subjected to unwelcome sexual intercourse while attending a college in the United States, numerous happen at or after parties. The majority of sexual assaults involve alcohol.

Many male students systematically use the party circumstances to coerce or manipulate women into sex. Recognizing the procedures of these rapists can help you avoid them.

Alcohol. They use alcohol or date rape drugs to weaken women's ability to resist sex. Also, they seek out drunk women because if they testify assaults, possible they will lack credibility, and others will be unable to remember the night's facts clearly.

Be careful with men who pressure you to drink or very eager about getting you a drink. Don't leave your drink unattended.
Split friends. These rapists try to split women away from their friends. Prepare plans with friends to stick together. Stay in public places or seating area, and very importantly, stay out of private quarters.

Disorientation. These kinds of students rapists targets women who are disoriented, and try to manipulate women into unfamiliar situations. Always know where you are, and the way to get home. Don't take a ride somewhere, not knowing how to get home.

Trust your instincts. If a guy gives you the impression of a creep, he almost definitely is a creep. You don't have to be pleasant to him. Don't be polite to a guy who is making you uncomfortable.

Forty-four U.S. states currently have anti-hazing laws
Six states (Alaska, Hawaii, Montana, New Mexico, South Dakota and Wyoming) do not have an anti-hazing law, compared to the 44 states that do. These anti-hazing laws are set in place to protect victims and punish those who are responsible.

If you are suspicions or have fears call your campus police or call 911.

Sexting

Sexting is a term use about sex-related or nude photos taken and shared via cell phone. That is not unlawful when done with consenting adults, when minors are involved, sexual-exploitation and child-pornography, there are strong laws that protect children.

Motives for sexting vary from seducing, sexual manipulation, to dating exploitation or blackmail.

There are two types of harassment:

Sexting as sexual harassment. Once somebody applies intimidation or extortion to get nude or sexually explicit photos from another person that is sexual harassment.

Sexting is an act out of anger, revenge or social assault. Exposing intimacy photos of someone without his or her approval are a violation that will cause emotional agony to an individual.

Another type of sexting is called experimental; it consists of no malice, or lack of permission between the two individuals. Most of the time there is no arrest or indictment.

Sextortion

Sextortion, this crime of extortion consist of sex-related digital photos. Demand money, sex, from the person, and threatening to release photos of him or her if the demand isn't met.
What to do if someone's sharing your nude photos?

There are laws against sexual harassment, stalking, wiretapping, and extortion, when adults are involved.

If the young person is underage 18, child sexual exploitation and child pornography law are in place to protect the teenager. Child-pornography laws are severe consequences for perpetrators.

In many districts, school staff must report child sexual abuse. As soon as a student reports to a teacher about sexting photos, the teacher by law is required to report that information to law enforcement.

What to do if you are a victim.

1-Ask a lawyer or counselor for advice.

2-Request photos on the website to be taken down – make use of the site abuse-reporting system.

3- Fill a report with the police or other law enforcement in your area.

Men's fraternity info

The men fraternities' topic is beyond the scope of this book, Because of the importance, we are going to give you some basic safe information.

For a student joining a fraternity means they will be accepted on campus, and have a group of friends, for students who arrive at school alone with no social group, this is important. Entering a fraternity may sound good, there are dangerous risks associated with it.

The analysis has revealed that fraternity men are at higher risk for perpetrating sexual assault due to their alcohol drinking, sexual attitude and group positions toward women.

More students engaged in drinking in a fraternity house than any other on-campus location. Harvard School of Public Health's College Alcohol Study, assert 75% of students residing in fraternity house were heavy drinkers, contrasted to 45% of students who live in non-Greek housing and 35% of the general student.

According to an article published in the journal Addiction, fraternity members are more prone to abuse prescription stimulants than the rest of the student's population.

Forty-four U.S. states currently have anti-hazing laws, six states, Alaska, Hawaii, Montana, New Mexico, South Dakota and Wyoming do not have an anti-hazing law, contrasted to the 44 states that do.

Historically, white fraternities are known for using alcohol in hazing rituals and black fraternities typically use physical violence.

Approximately 130 individuals were injured or killed as a result of hazing from 1923-1980, although the real numbers are much higher especially in the 90s' and 2000s. Initiates should be aware of the danger of hazing.

Often, young men pledge a fraternity with no knowledge they may be beaten, sexually abused, forced to drink liquor, locked naked in the trunk of a car, or other tortuous hazing events that take place.

If pledges were aware of the amount of tortuous pledges they will be exposed to it would surely drop because one's life and dignity is not worth trading for some brother's friends.

It is far better to be alone, than to be in bad company
George Washington

Common mistakes women make

1-When the attacker orders you into the car pointing a gun or a knife. The attackers don't want to shoot you; they want you to get into the car so that they can drive you to a deserted place and rape you. **Don't**. Run screaming. It is much more likely than not that he will just move on to an easier target.

2. Stopping over when a man drives alongside of you pointing at your car pretending something is wrong.

Never **pull over**; many women have been raped because of this.

3. Keeping unlocks doors while driving.

The attacker simply walks up to a woman's car while she's at a **traffic light** and **jumps** in with his gun or knife drawn.

4. Opening the front door when you don't know who is knocking.

If you don't have a **peep hole**, get **one**. I've seen countless cases where the attacker gains access to his victims simply by knocking on their door.

5. Don't let an attacker get **into your home**. He then has a private, relatively soundproof place to attack you for hours.

To help the police work

1. Keep a **record** of all events, telephone calls, etc., documenting as much detail as possible including the time and date of incidents.

2. Try to get **evidence** of your stalker's actions like a photograph or video.

3. Do not **throw away** parcels or letters from the stoker. Handle them with **care** and as little as possible, place them in plastic sleeves or envelopes to **preserve** them.

4. You **should read** any mail you receive in case it contains threats or indecent / offensive language. Is not the nicest thing to do, but you must **know** what is going on and have an idea of the **stacker mind**, places and actions he is **thinking** about .

Identifying the criminal

Sex	Race	Scar
Age	Tattoos (very	Defect
Accent	important)	Wound
Cloth	Hair color	
Weapon use if any	Height	

Better a thousand times careful than once dead
Proverb

Chapter 6-Purse snatching

Purse snatching is a crime of **opportunity**. Eliminate that opportunity. A female carrying a purse is a target for this kind of crime. A woman carrying a purse strap over her shoulder's is a potential target. Especially when they are older citizens they make the perfect victims for thieves because he thinks they can't defend themselves.

What must you do?

Most purse snatchers are young people looking for easy and a fast way to make money.

Try not to **expose** your wallet in the open; this is the **first** precaution you can take. Try to keep some money or credit card in your pant, one or two pockets if necessary. Credit cards, driver's license and your car keys should be carried in a coat or jean pocket so you don't have to open your wallet.

Out-think the Purse Snatcher

Do not wrap the strap around your shoulder or neck. Purse snatch victims have been thrown down and drag on the floor and have been badly hurt. Every woman makes this mistake; they place the purse on a store counter. Never ever do this. You must listen, never do this.

Should I let him take my purse?

A decision like this, you have to make at the moment and very fast, and that decision is yours.
I think if the criminal wants to get just your purse, just let him have it. Your life is more important than anything else. Don't you think so?

You must

It is a must keep copies at home of the credit cards you are carrying, know where and how to report stolen credit cards. Also, is a good idea not to carry much cash. Just in case.

Here are some suggestions

1. Keep an eye on your surroundings. Look people in the eye.

2. Go shopping with a friend is an excellent idea.

3. Don't go shopping at night if possible, it is more dangerous.

4. Avoid parking garages if possible, park close to the store if you have the opportunity.

5. If your purse is snatched, let them take your purse. It is not worth getting hurt.

6. Leave your **Social Security card** at home; this information gives great information for identity theft.

7. Carry one or two credit cards with you.

8 .Very good idea is to keep at home a list of the credit cards and all the information about them.

Keep a log home

Credit card #- Type of card: Visa, American express- Name of the bank.

Contact # to cancel the card if it is stolen.

9. In case your cell is stolen, you will need this information

Cell phone #- Company name-Model number/ name-The Serial #

10. Never leave your purse, bag or briefcase in your car visible, don't leave anything that a criminal may think is valuable, and place it in the trunk.

You can prevent these attacks when you take the opportunity away from the thief, or better yet when he looks at you and see no opportunity in your person.

Peace is its own reward
Mahatma Gandhi

Children

Protecting Children

Protecting children is a scope out of this book. Because of the importance we are going to go over it lightly.

Useful tips:

1. Think of a **"family password"** just in case anyone picks the kids up at school "since Mommy or Daddy'' could not make it, that person MUST give them the family password or the child should **not leave** with them. **Period**.

2. Let them know of about others **kids** defending **themselves.**

3. I read in the news of a girl who was walking home from school when she was approached by a predator and had trouble running away because she was afraid to lose her schoolbooks, fearing that her father would be angry at her if she lost the books. It is very important that **kids understand** that all those rules are **suspended** if they are in **personal danger!!! Tell them over and over.**

4. Teach them to **scream,** really **loud** if they are in **danger**. If someone covers their mouth, teach them to **kick** and **scratch** areas such as **groin, eyes, throat** and **knees, bites the ear or nose if necessary.** Teach them to **scream, scream, scream.**

5. Do not write in backpacks and clothing the **child's name visible**. This is definitely not a good idea, a stranger may call your child by name, and kids are not suspicious of a person who knows their name and provably respond to the predator, they may think this person must be a friend because he/she knows them by name. See the **danger**?

6. Have your children's fingerprints taken and store safely. Make sure your children know their phone number and address.

7. Keep a current photograph of your child.

One of the key tips for criminals are honor roll bumper stickers, the criminal knows where your child goes to school. A criminal could find your child this way.

A cell phone it is a great device for a responsible child, but it can be a risky problem, if they are walking from school or to school, in the park or playground, likely they are not paying attention to their surroundings. You likewise must monitor children's Cyber activity; teach them what to look out for.

Threats to children are evolving common over the Internet; you must give them advice on how to stay safe.

Talk to your child about what they would do if someone grabs them. Explain they must act.
Stand up for your child's decision not to hug or kiss a relative, uncle, cousin. Maybe is for a reason.

Accompany your children to a public restroom, or wait for them by the door and monitor the length of time they are there. If suspicious of the time yell for them or just walk in.
The National Center of Exploited Children confirms that less than 1% of all reported cases of child abductions under the age of 18 in the United States are perpetrated by a family member or acquainted of the children's family.

Child Fear Response

Dry mouth	Screaming
Sobbing	Sweaty hands
Yelling	Mumbling
Quivering	

Teach them to scream "I don't know you." "Leave me alone."

Kids Internet Safety

The Internet has changed how children spend time, instead of playing outside; the Internet also present's new dangers like.

1-Cyberbullying
2-Exposure to indecent information
3-Sex predators
4-Exposing private information

Basic tips for children using the Internet

A-Computer should be kept in a high-traffic section of your home.
B-Supervise cell phones, gaming, gadgets, and laptops.
C-Learn who is connecting with your children, online with.

A child miseducated is a child lost
John F. Kennedy

Lessen your chances of being a victim

Attitude

A- Having the right attitude
B- Develop **Security Awareness**

Your mind is the utmost defensive defense. The more **confident** you appear, the better off you are.

A-Use **common sense** at all times
B- Trust your **instincts**.
C- Weapons: **Attitude, Awareness** and Voice

Use your intuition:

A-Be confident and clever to deal with the situation.
B-Verbalize! Leave me alone! Or "Get away from me!"
C- Face a potential attacker. Don't turn your back. Back away from him.
D-Don't bring strangers home. Don't go any place, home, with an unfamiliar person.
E-Chance routine as much as possible, try not to come home or go to work at the same time every day.

Learning some **defense tactics**
Types of Self-defense

Physical approach:

A-Natural weapons of defense-your voice, body and actions.
B-Men have weak areas- Women learn to strike at the groin, Adam's apple, the eyes and ears.
C- Pepper Spray-Time is of greatest importance. When something tells you to act-Act.
Don't pull out your spray until you are ready to use it! Make sure you will hit your attacker right in the face.

Cane defense

Most people with mobility conditions with injuries or physical incapacity uses a cane. If you need to carry one, you can use it to defend yourself. The more suitable, effortlessness and undemanding your defense must be.

I am just mentioning some of the simple and easy to do defenses you could use. Nothing complicated, confusing, especially if you rely on a cane for mobility.

High strikes

Block a punch with the cane.
The head- sideways, down strike.
The eyes
The neck-sideways, front strike
The windpipe-sideways, front strike
A thrust to the chest

Low strikes

A strike up the groin.
The knees, front smack or sideways strike

Strike the legs, the shins, a strike here is difficult to block.
The knees, lower legs, or the shins are ideal targets since they are easy to hit and difficult for the aggressor to defend. When you hurt his legs you halt his ability to chase you when you run away.

It may sound too simple for you, but a cane is a potent weapon for self-defense. The attacker was hoping for an easy victim; you gave him the surprise of his life! It works in your favor.
As you aged your skills decline, you have to modify your protection to yours specific physical requirements. However, you can always defend yourself.

Injustice anywhere is a threat to justice everywhere
Martin Luther King, Jr.

Self-Defense Tactics for Women

People think that if a muscular man attack you, you could not hurt him, right? Not true, you can. He likes everyone else has weak points his eyes are vulnerable to finger jabs or a pen, pencil or your keys.

If the attack is made from the back, and he holds you with his arm around your neck you should turn your chin toward the elbow of the attacker and force it down to relieve pressure against the windpipe. Lock the chin down; try to keep the attacker's forearm from pressing hard enough against the side of the neck that unconsciousness could occur. Then, the eyes should be attacked over the shoulder, groin grabbed, or top of the instep stomped with the heel. Move quickly, forward, sideways or backward, do not hesitate hitting him with the back of your head, one, twice, as many times as you can, go for his eyes, ears, lips.

Grab the groin or hit it to make an attacker loosen a physical hold on you, hit back him with the elbows to his solar plexus or over the shoulder to the attacker's face.
The worst nightmare is for you to wake up in bed and find an attacker in your face. If you decide to fight, using a combination of yelling try to jab his eyes, scratch his eyes, cheeks, run, people who fight get away from attackers much more than people who offer no resistance.

The statistic shows that those who fight get broken fingers, injured black eyes, and the likes. About 55% of the people who offer no resistance get injured anyway.

Many times it is smarter to not resist, could be the correct choice for self-defense. Like when an attacker is threatening the life of your children, or he has a gun or knife, this place you in a situation where maybe is safer to do what he says - that's okay. You and only you can decide in a particular situation.

The real key to this encounter is you **deciding in a split of a second what to do**. Remember, any object you can hit him with on the face, eyes, this will give you some time to escape. Again, it is **your decision** and only yours.

Attacks occur more during the transitions where you are going from one place to another. Think about that. Traveling in your car to work or work to your home, it also takes place walking to the parking lot, many times taking out the trash, or jogging early morning or late afternoon. I do not agree with what many experts think about the safe of walking with small dogs, in my opinion walking with a dog or small child increases your risk of attack. Why? Your attention is focused in seating your child on the booster seat or in securing the child with the seatbelts.

The next time you will see a lady unloading or loading the kids in the car pay attention and you will see what I mean.

Your decision to fight on depends on if you are alone, with kids, your physical condition, how far you are from help, or people. If help is closed by, you may want to make a commotion, noises, throw anything you can rocks, bags, clothes into the attacker's face and run and yell.

The only mistake in life is the lesson not learned
Albert Einstein

Female Police force Tips

1-Women should keep a pepper spray for safety.

2- the spray away from children.

3-<u>Test</u> it after you purchased it.

4-Testing your spray regularly is absolutely important. You want to make sure it works at any time.

5-You must verify how far and the direction the spray will go.

6-If you use it; yell "stop" sprout the pepper spray at the assailant's face.

7-Pepper spray needs a few instants to produce an effect, and you may want to spray again, and move away and run if possible.

8-Permanently keep your Pepper Spray in the same place to make sure it reachable.

For safety is not a gadget but a state of mind
Eleanor Everet

MAKE AWARENESS PART OF YOUR LIFE

Some people feel they are becoming paranoid when they practice awareness. However, you should with time develop it into a natural habit. It is very crucial to pay attention to all times to your surroundings. It could save your life.

AWARENESS YOU SHOULD PRACTICE AND WORK ON IT AT HOME

1. **Write only** initials and last name in the phone book, doors, mailboxes. **Add** another name if you live alone.

2. **Be careful** when you give out your information in public. A delinquent could use this information.

3. If you are on **vacation** do not leave notes in your door, have a friend pick the mail so it won't be obvious that nobody is home , invest in a good timer and have it on like from 7:00pm to 11:00 pm if possible do the same with a radio a couple of times also in the daytime.

4. Entrance doors, back doors, including your garage should be **well lighted**. Keep the garage door shut and **locked** all the time.

5. Use **timers** in various parts of the house to activate lights at **different times thru the night.**

6. **Install an alarm,** also is a good idea to have **a dog** because it will alert you if any noise. Don't rely on dogs 100%; there have been times when they have been poisoned by criminals.

7. If somebody is trying to **break in** or you **hear noises,** turn on all outside lights and call the police. Do not hesitate. Don't ever **go out** to check. Sometimes they use this tactic to get you to come out, get you by surprise and get asset to you and your house. Never ever **go outside**.

They are spec ting where you are coming out; you don't know where they are hiring. **Call the police**.

8. At **night,** especially you should keep windows, doors, curtains closed and shades down.

9. **A tactic** commonly used by many rapists is a **visit unannounced**, they know the victims are alone or very busy and plan the time of the attack. Don't take unexpected visit, do not open the door. Tell them through the window to come back another day because you are expecting company. Don't be shy, **do it**.

10. **Do not open the door** to service personnel, especially, if you have not requested service, ask for the office phone number thru behind the door, and call the office to verify. A child's opening the door is a no. Never ever allow it.

11. Don't leave house **keys** in places like under doormats, in flower boxes. You better believe it, burglars know where to **look.**

12. If someone **knocks at your door** to ask you to use the phone because of an emergency. Don't go for that trick, again ask them thru the close door who you will call, call yourself or better yet, call the police and let them help, maybe you call an **accomplice Beware.**

13. Do not **open the door** to deliveries unless you know the delivery person or you know you are expecting a delivery from a company.

14. **Bushes** should be trim so no one can hide in them, keep bushes away from the front door and garage door. Shrubs are notorious for camouflaging basement windows. Bushes give provide coverage for a thief to break in, giving them a lot of time.

Think of places an attacker could hide, both inside and outside. Security bars are a good system, it will make it harder to breakin. Numerous individuals use security film. If the window is hit by a rock, the glass will be stuck in place by the film. Impeding easily gains access to your home! Keep chairs and tables that can be used to climb, away from the windows. Complicating his way, your home will be a lot safer.

15. If you use an apartment laundry, wait to be with someone. Make plans with another person you know in the building and do it together. Do not spend unnecessary time alone in the room. Get in and get out. Don't spend any more time in there that you need to. If you have to do it alone, change the days of the week and time you do it so a rapist can't make a plan. Always look around before stepping inside.

16- Never allow mail to be addressed to you with salutations like Miss, Mrs., and MS, Make them nondescript as to your sex and marital status.

17-Avoid using stairs if you live in an apartment.

18- Change the lock right away when moving to a new house/ apartment.

19-Make sure to secure glass doors with braces

20-Never leave ladders or high chairs against your house.

21-Practice using your phone in the dark

Yell fire instead of help, most people will run out of their apartment.

AWARENESS IN YOUR CAR

1. When you walk to your car in a parking lot, as you approach the car give a glare underneath to see if anyone is hiding behind.

2. Look inside your car before getting in.

4. Buy a cell phone; make sure that is always charged

5. Your gas tank should always be full or half full.

6. All valuables must be out of view and locked in the trunk.

7. If you have to pull over and stop on a street, try to pull over to a business that is open 24 hours, stay in the car and use your cell phone to make your calls. It is okay to use the public phone from the store, but if the phone is in a dark area or is not inside the store, go inside and ask to use the store's phone. By all mean do not use one in a dark corner away from people.
 If someone offers help, roll the window ½ an inch and ask them to call the police.

8. Park in well-lit areas as close as possible to the place you are visiting and approach your car with your keys already ready in your hands.

9. If a van has parked next to your car, be careful, better to enter your car from the other side. Vans are frequently used to kidnap.

10. When you stop at a red light at night or a lonely street keep your car in gear with doors locked and windows rolled up.

11. Be familiar with your routes and vary your route home if possible.

12. If someone signals that something is wrong, do not stop to check your car, later when the other car is gone, stop in a populated parking lot and check.

13. Keep an extra home key with you so you can leave the keys with a parking attendant or gas station without leaving your house key with it. It takes a few minutes to make a copy.

14. Never pick up a hitchhiker, male or female.

15. Carjacking happens in places with a high trust level for the driver.

16. When driving, notice the cars around you. At night be careful not being blocked on either side or from the front and the rear.

17. Do not drive in the far right-hand lane on unfamiliar streets so as not to be easily approached at stop lights. Travel the middle lanes.

Very important

18. Always stop far enough away from the car in front of you. This will give you enough room to maneuver your car out in an emergency. I always see so many people stop so close to the car in front, it's crazy if an emergency comes up they can get out.

19. If an aggressor demands your car, and there is no chance to accelerate and escape, give it right ways, just tell him, let me take my kid out and right away get out and begin taking the kid out while you are giving him the keys.
Don't wait for his approval to take the kids out, just do it.

20. Always be defensive and keep your eyes open.

21. Buy a call police sign.

22. Never park next to a man sitting just in his car

23. In a convertible never drive at night by yourself with the top down and in places you don't know.

24. Lock the door and start your car, move and only then when you are in a position that allows you to drive forward lock your safety belt, or look at your package if you must. I repeat your car should be in a position so you could drive away if you must.

This is one of the mistakes I see women doing all the time.

Life is like riding a bicycle. To keep your balance, you must keep moving.

Albert Einstein

Phone Precautions

1. List your initials and your last name in the phone book only.

2. In your answering machine if you live alone, ask for a male friend to record for you and he should say something to the like we are not in. Never use I'm not here.

3. Don't tell anyone that you are alone. If you need to, said your brother, husband or boyfriend is taking a shower.

4. If you are the focus of an obscene call. Hang up right away. Take your phone off for a while, hang it up again after 20 minutes or so. The person is going to get tired.

5. When you get a wrong call number don't tell them your phone number. When the person asks you for it, ask them what number they were trying to reach. Confirmed the mistake, but do not tell him your phone.

6. Keep Police, fireman, boyfriend, brother or friends' telephone numbers handy and close by the phone.

Don't ever leave your guard down!

Tips in the street

1. Walk with your head up and with a steady pace.

2. If you are a woman, avoid walking through a group of men or young guys.

3. Walk in well lighted streets with a lot of traffic. Avoid walking by bushes, alleys, and never take shortcuts through deserted places. Change your route home once in a while.

4. If you assumed that someone or if you are being followed, cross the street, cross it back after a few minutes after you just cross it, change directions, this way the predator knows you are aware and probably because he doesn't want people to notice the situation and if someone is washing it is obvious there is a problem he would leave.

5. Hold your purse or bags firm. If the robber demanded your purse, tossed it to him, choose your own safety before your purse.

6. Try to keep your hands free as possible as you can. Never allow force or threats to get you into a car. **Never ever!** Whatever it is going to happen, let it happen, in front of everybody. If you take this advice you are going to be 99% safer than if you let them take you somewhere else.

7. If you have to wait outside for somebody, be aware of cars that pull up to you or if they pass you repeatedly. Keep your eyes open.

8. If a car stops and the driver asks you for directions, you don't have to answer, if you do answer, do not get close to the car. Tell him from far away.

9. Don't ever accept rides from strangers, never take one from one.

10. If you have to use public transportation like a bus, train or subway, sit as close to the driver and to the front as possible, don't let people know ahead of time with any kind of clue as where you are going to get off, stand at the last moment to do so, be aware of the people getting off with you. When riding the bus or subway never sleep.

11. Stay away from lonely streets, stay away from alleys and parked cars.

12. Never take a shortcut

13. Avoid badly lit stairways and bus stop

14. Don't show money in public

15. Keep your wallet in your front pocket, especially when traveling to avoid being pocketed.

16. If you are wearing high heel shoes and being followed, get rid of them so you can run

17. Learn your subway and bus schedule so you don't have to be waiting more than necessary.

18.Vary your travel route.

19. When biking, jogging or walking is a most to stay away from deserted places and keep your eyes alert and ears with no music or gadget.

20. Try to walk in the contrary traffic direction.

21. Be very cautious in public restrooms all the time.

22. Before entering a fast convenience store, take a few seconds to look before you do enter if it is late at night.

23. When walking in unfamiliar buildings look around as you walk and notice where the exit doors are located.

24. Don't stop to talk to the unfamiliar person in the streets.

25. Avoid streets and restroom where a group of teenagers is congregated.

26. When grocery shopping keep your purse in sight.

27. Never sit with your back to the entrance or public in restaurants or public places. Unfortunate I learned from this mistake many years ago and since then I have never ever sat with my back to the public or entrance ever again.

Everyone should avoid loneliness –dark places

True peace is not merely the absence of tension: it is the presence of justice

Martin Luther King Jr

Keep in mind thoughts

A- Fighting just to **preserve** your "honor" from verbal attack is not a smart thing to do.

B-In the law's eyes you can only retaliate if you felt you or a family member were going to get hurt or die.

C-In real life, practically no one will ever attack you the way it's demonstrated in 99% martial art schools.

D-Every additional second you are in contact with your attacker, you are closer to dying... or getting badly hurt.

E-If you fight a guy in the street or bar, you can be sure you will be fighting his friends as well. If this takes place prepare to be stomped to death. **Every added second** you fight you are vulnerable to more assailants.

F- If in the process of fighting you **maim or kill** your aggressor, the process with the police is huge and you will have to live with that the rest of your life. It is not an easy thing to do.

G- Inform yourself about your rights in your state. Learn about the law's view of the use of force.

You must **avoid** all fights at all costs. Priority # one is to get out, escape. Fight only when you think you or a family member is going to be hurt or kill. Not humiliated or offended.

You must not hesitate to use the following technique if an emergency comes up:

A-Butting with the head, sideways, upward, downward. Any way you can.

C-**Biting**-neck-ear, shoulder-arms-hand-legs even fingers. Make sure to split any blood, he may be sick or infected.

D- **Hair puling**-head-chest-arms.

E- **Groin attack**.

F- **Striking** downward, upward or sideways using the point of the elbow.

G-**Throat strikes** especially the trachea.

H-**Eye gouging**.

I- **Lips pulling**, sideways, up or down.

J- **Pulling, bending**, even braking fingers, especially the little one.

I don't initiate violence, I retaliate
Chuck Norris

Canine attacks

I want to mention about dogs attacks, these pass two months I have wittiness three different occasions and locations where people walking their dogs, were attacked by dogs that escaped from their homes and attacked these dogs walking with their owners in a Leash. One happened two houses away from my house, the noise and commotion was immense. I try to intervene and help this person, being very careful. The dog at any moment could have diverted the attack toward me.

Dogs as you know have been called men best friends, most people when they think of a dog thinks of a passive and trusty dog. However, there have been multiple attacks occurrences, particularly, if you are walking with a smaller dog or exercising on the streets.

You must be alert of the area when walking through an unknown zone. Dogs are territorial and could feel restless when a stranger, particularly, with another dog enters their territory.

If a dog moves towards you in an angry manner, barking, and growling, this is a sign of a hostile dog.

If you are able to, cross over to an alternative street. If not, try to whistle, or talk in a non-threatening manner. Don't run; stop moving, as long as the dog is close by. Don't wave your arms; running will activate the dog's natural instinct to pursue the prey.

Remain still and calm, don't make eye contact, staring down is not advised, the dog could sense you as weak, stand tall so you can seem bigger.

When the dog calm down, move slowly backward, and backward until you are far away from the dog, then very slowly walk away.

If the dog attacks, you must attempt to reduce the damage by generating some kinds of obstacle between you and the dog. Pick a street trash can lid to use as a shield, anything, a rock to hit it. A backpack is also a great barrier.

If you have nothing to use as a barrier and find there is no alternative, remove your shirt or coat and wrap it around your arm. This way you are providing the dog an object to bite while lessening the wound otherwise the dog will inflict on you.

Don't under any circumstance, let the dog drag you to the floor, your chances of surviving are minimal. Strike the eyes, the nose, the legs, many times, over and over again, dogs have a thick skull. While yelling for help.

After the Attack

1-Call 911 right away.

2-Get to a doctor immediately, you may get an antibiotics or tetanus shot, if there is a doubt the dog may have had rabies, some rabies shots.

3-Identify the dog-this will help the doctor determine if you need Rabies shots.

4-Confirm if the dog is a pet or a stray dog.

5-You may need to speak to a lawyer, to dispute you and the owner.

Even if the animal bike seems insignificant, infections can quickly become infected. Seek medical attention right away,

There have been only a few cases of people surviving rabies infections after onset of symptoms.

Chapter 7-Identity Theft

Every four seconds someone becomes a victim of identity theft. Today this is one of the most lucrative crimes, reason? It is done from a distance and most of the time the victim won't realize he is being victimized for a month at least.

Protect your identity

You must guard your identity at all cost. Approximately 10 million Americans have been victims of Id theft. Of the ten million about half only knew their identity was stolen.

Your identity is stolen in different ways.

Stealing your purse or wallet. Obtaining name, address, even social security.

Dumpster looking-Picking up bank account numbers, company you deal with, credit cards offer, bills.

Breaking into your house and stilling vital information. Bank checks, credit cards, bills.

Breaking into your computer-Confidential information, loans, credit card numbers, and companies you deal with.

Credit Bureau-Posing as an employer or company to steal your information.

Shoulder looking-to steal your PIN at the ATM and then creating a similar card and use your pin.

Scamming-they try for you to tell them you social security using different tricks, they do it by e-mail, phone call or even by visiting you or by posing as someone else.

Take action now!

Take action now

You should shred all your information, including your child too.
Make a point to check credit card statement all the time.

Pay attention at the ATM or bank.
Use difficult password and change them every six months.
Protect your social security at all cost. Don't give it out without
asking why they need it. Make sure they really need it.

Carry two credit cards at one time.
Don't ever give personal information over the phone, internet or by
mail.
Birth Certificate, Social Security card, Passport and important record,
must be Storage in a safe.

 Shop only at secure websites.
Do not use a debit card when you shop online
ever. If anything happens when you are using a
credit card your legal responsibility is around
$50.00 only vs. a debit card, which is about
$500.00. Do you understand?

If you suspect anything act fast

Contact the Mayor Credit Bureaus
Close down all accounts.
File a police report

Try to remember which company asks you lately for information
about you.
Call and report the situation to all the companies you deal with.

There is no infallible foolproof against this kind of hacker. Your best
defense is to keep your guard up to lower your risk so you won't
become a victim of identity theft.
 Suspect anything. Act immediately; if you are suspicious something
is wrong.

Samples of States Identity Theft

The Consumer Sentinel Network received over 3 million complaints in 2016 of identity theft. This crime rose, from 246,214 in 2006 to 399,225 in 2016.

The Federal Trade Commission's 2017 Consumer Sentinel Network Data reviewed the states with the most and least identity theft. Also, considered were total identity theft complaints, fraud complaints per 100,000 residents, and the average amount stolen by a scammer. All figures are for 2016 and were obtained from the FTC's report.

1. Arizona-Identity theft 100,000: 126.2

2. Nevada-Identity theft complaints per 100,000: 135.8

3. Missouri-Identity theft complaints per 100,000: 136.1

4. Maryland-Identity theft complaints per 100,000: 137.1

5. Connecticut-Identity theft complaints per 100,000: 137.9

6. Illinois-Identity theft complaints per 100,000: 138.0

7. California-Identity theft complaints per 100,000: 139.5

8. Delaware-Identity theft complaints per 100,000: 155.9

9. Florida-Identity theft complaints per 100,000: 166.8

10. Michigan-Identity theft complaints per 100,000: 175.6

How does credit card get stolen?

5 places it can occur:

1. At the pump
You're fueling up for your trip; someone else could be grabbing your credit card number. Watch out for suspicious card-reading devices attached right over legitimate ones, like at a gas station or ATM, to steal your info.

2. Coffee shop
The WI-FI network that looks like it's the coffee shops may actually be a fake. Credit card numbers you send while you're logged in could be easily collected. To protect the info you're sharing and make it harder to steal, make sure you're using an encrypted network.

3. In your inbox
You may have heard of "phishing," These common scams can arrive by email, text or social media message. You will see a request for your credit card or Social Security number from what seems to be a familiar site, like a well-known store or bank. If you reply, you will be giving thieves exactly what they're looking for.

4. On the phone
A lady called saying she's trying to help solve an unusual charge on your card. She needs you to confirm your credit card number to make the fix. It's called "vishing" (voice phishing) you don't want to fall for it. No matter how credible she sounds, avoid giving your account number or other personal information over the phone unless you made the call.

5. At the wayside
If you dump credit card statements, receipts in the recycling without shredding them first, you could be giving "Dumpster divers" an opportunity to turn your garbage into gold.

Staying aware of the threats that are out there might just stop a bad guy from get hold of your credit card number. Keep those cards and numbers safe.

Massive of phones rip-offs are done each year, mainly on the elderly

The crooks take advantage of Senior citizens and make them selected to rip-off artists, thugs and crooks.

Federal officials will never make any unsolicited contact via telephone, email, fax, or front door visit asking for money or personal, financial information, including your social security. They also try to get your medical history to steal your social security.

Scammers may create website intended to look like official sites. States website's should end with "gov". Scare or rush tactics indicate you are dealing with a scammer. Safeguard your personal and medical history, no matter what you're being offered in return.

Look out points

A- Free vacation and prices-The caller asks you to pay the taxes, to pay for delivery. Ask you or try to make you buy better room, hotel or early departure. A complete red flag is free vacation, trips. If you really won anything you shouldn't have to pay for it.

B- E-mail and websites. These scammers make you believe that your computer is at risk, by asking you to give information and or to download malicious software, so they can steal your information.

C- The lotto ticket-very old scam-Many people still getting ripped with it. You know how it goes, they approach you in the store, and then ask you if you want to exchange a million dollar ticket because they are undocumented. If you give them xxx amount of money, they give it to you. Every month elderly people fall for this scam. Please don't.

D- Loan scams-If you get a call from a company that wants to loan you money. It is a scam. They offer you money and ask you all the information that they can take out of you, especially bank account numbers, credit card number with the excuse to have it file so you can pay the loan back. Reputable Loan Company doesn't make these kinds of calls. Hang up immediately.

E-IRS-You receive a call telling you to pay xx-xx amount of money right away, or they are going to arrest you. Sometimes they leave a message on your answering machine, you call back, and someone answers IRS may I help you- Then they transfer your call to someone who claim to be an agent working on your case, then try to get all the money they can from you, using all kinds of scare tactics. Old folks fall for this scam all the time.

Hang your phone right away. The IRS, never calls you, they sent you a letter through the USPS. Even if you ever get a letter, make sure to check is real and not a scam before taking any action.

F-Car accident-This one is of the latest scam. They have someone call you and tell you, your wife, or husband or son or daughter has been in an accident. If you don't pay a xx-xx amount of money right away, they are going to jail. Sometimes they even put on the phone a woman or a man crying (it depends) begging, so the person receiving the call is under stress, afraid, and confuse, with the person on the phone crying and the voice alter, can't really tell if it is her daughter, son or wife. Many older people are victims of this one. Be careful, hang the phone right away.

Be alert always!

Medical Identity Theft

Identity theft is typically related with monetary transactions. Medical theft happens when someone uses another individual name or insurance data to get medical treatment, prescription, and drugs. Also, it occurs with corrupt people employed in the medical setting use personal information to summit bogus bills to insurance organizations.

You should assume you are a victim if you receive:

A bill for medical examinations you did not receive.
If you are contacted by a debt collector for a medical debt you did not owe.
If you see a medical collection notification on your credit report you don't recognize.
You are told by your health plan you have reached your limit benefit.
Denied insurance for the reason that records show a condition you do not have.

As a patient you have the right to have your medical and billing records corrected. The law authorizes a one free photocopy from each provider and health plans every 12 months.
You have the right to file a complaint if you think your privacy rights have been violated.

Everyone should check their social security number, address, name, and employee's names to be sure they are listed correctly. If you notice incorrect information, visit FTC.Gov/idtheft to correct it. The FTC works to stop fraudulent and unfair practices and help consumers how to prevent them.

If you need extra information visits FTC.Gov/idtheft.

Act fast-the faster you act the better

The Street fighter advantage over you is clear, no doubt about it. The street fighter will try to sucker punch you and throw many punches and surprises with fast blows with no plans whatsoever. He probably will use only a few techniques, but he is very good at them.

My advice and that of many knowledge fighters is to keep your technique simple, fast uncomplicated and move as much and fast as you can. Move sideways or back and then move, move and move Just move!!

Actuality the best technique is not to fight and get out of the situation, this is the most smart self-defense there it is. There are only a few reasons to risk being hurt and that is if your life or the lives of your loves ones are in danger. That is it. Nothing else is merit getting hurt for.

Here you have it, now it is up to you to practice awareness so you never get in a situation where you have to defend yourself or use the techniques and tactics if you have to, Good Luck.

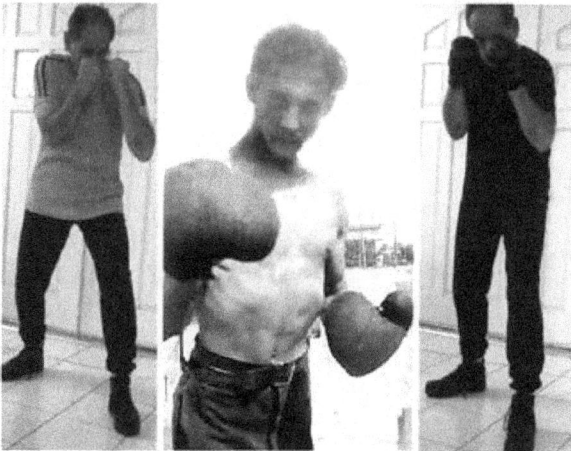

The Author with his father in the center, who taught him how to defend himself at a very young age, same thing he did with his son years later.

Like Father like son

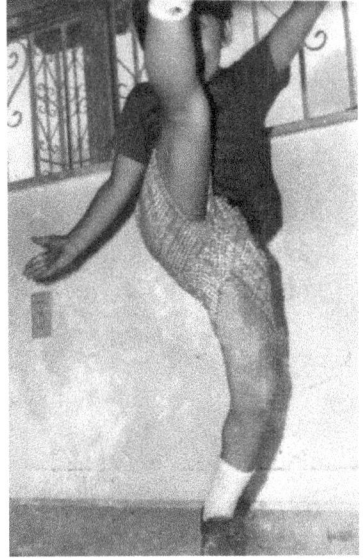

The Author doing a Front Kick   *Frank Jr. practicing a Front kick*

Practicing the front kick 38 years ago

The Author practicing   *taking a break from sparring*

Rear kick

Practicing with the Nunchaku

The Author practicing long time ago

The Author teaching his son how to use the Nunchaku.

Frank Jr. practicing at a very early age

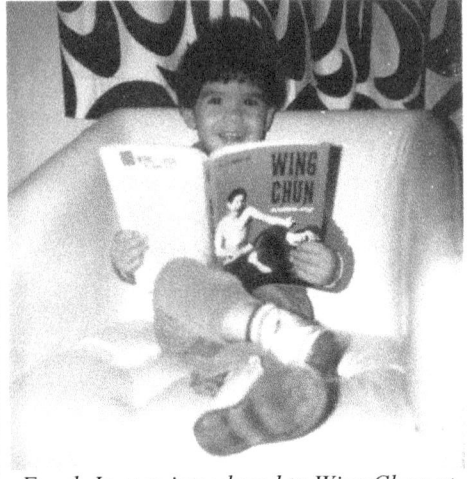

Frank Jr. was introduced to Wing Chun at a very young age

Practicing/Sparring

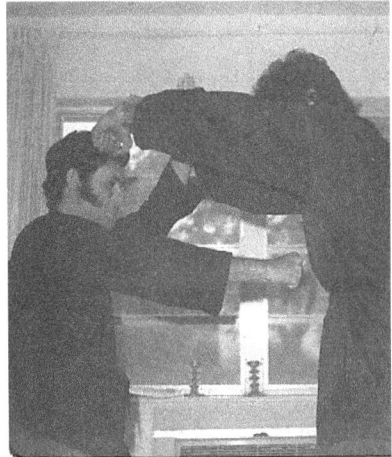

Practicing

Fast Punching

Meditating

The author, after some kind of "incident in Mexico City" left photo

The author after defending himself against a very numerous gang attack.

The Author sustained the boxer's fracture, "Brawler's Fracture" 3 times in his lifetime.

With the group Rat Patrol antique Car-after a gang attack

with his Ford Galaxy 500LX 1965

Mass Shooting surviving

If you hear gunfire and people are yelling, get out as quickly as you can. In a mass shooting, minutes matter, run away from the gunfire noise as fast as possible. Experts agree the safest action is to run away from the gunfire in the direction of an exit door. Don't run into offices or bathrooms where no way out is. Look for the side doors, patios or windows you can use to escape.

If you decide to hide, be quick in deciding where to hide, barricade yourself, and block the door with a filing cabinet, a desk or any heavy object. Stays away from doors, bullets go through doors. Don't turn the lights on, don't make any noise, if there is another person in the room, one person should call 911, then turn cell phones off, or place all phones in vibration, and don't talk to anyone else if you are hiding with someone. If you hear the attacker close by, don't call the authorities; don't take the risk for the shooter to hear you.

Without making any noise gather any weapons to attack the attacker if you have to, scissors, a pen, any object you could use. Fight if you have to, if the attacker is coming at you, and there is no way to escape, you must fight. Aim for the eyes, the face, nose, neck or crotch. Be aggressive. As soon as you can run in the direction of law enforcement, keep your hands above your head and keep your hands visible at all times, so they can tell you are not the attacker.

In a critical situation, lie on the floor face down. To protect your internal organs, in addition, if the shooter passes by you, he may think you're dead; the shooter won't waste bullets on someone who is dead. The only way to survive a Mass Shooting is to be always aware, and react fast, run and hide as fast as you can.

If you find yourself under lethal attack don't be kind. Be harsh. Be tough. Be ruthless.

Jeff Cooper

Terrorist

Homeland Security Advisory System

The Homeland Security Advisory System is a system for distributing information about the risk of terrorist acts to federal, state, local authorities and, through them to the mass media and to the public.

The system delivers warnings as the risk of an act of terrorism increases. Each threat sets protective procedures by the federal branches to decrease vulnerability, as suggestions to states and local governments. District officials will update the public if you need to take action where you live and work.

Terrorism use force or violence against people or property for the intention of intimidation, or ransom. Terrorists use aggression and threats to create fear in the public, and to obtain instant exposure for their causes.

Terrorism varies between threats, murders, abductions, commercial airline hijackings, car bombs, computer attacks, biochemistry, and nuclear weapons.

The five threat conditions are:

Low (green): low risk of terrorist attacks
Guarded (blue): general risk of terrorist attacks
Elevated (yellow): significant risk of terrorist attacks
High (orange): high risk of terrorist attacks
Severe (red): severe risk of terrorist attacks

Terrorist

FBI

Consulting the FBI law enforcement report the typical active shooter occurrence last 12 minutes, with 37% taking less than five minutes. Forty-three% of the time the confrontation is over before law enforcement appears on the scene.

Facing an active shooter, you don't want to wait until he closes you in, you don't want to place yourself in the direction of fire if you can prevent it. Your goal should be staying out of the line of fire, use cover.

Scenario tactic:

Stay out of the fire line.

Cover and hide

If you must approach the shooter do it from the side or rear

Use speed, surprise and intense aggression.

Use all sorts of strikes

Aim firearm muzzle to the attacker.

Stop the aggressor by any needed means

Stay out of the fire line, cover and hide

"Defeat is not defeat unless accepted as a reality-in your own mind."

Bruce Lee

Terrorism

Lessening Terrorist Violence Begins with you

The most significant skill is to become more vigilant of our surroundings. We can use our common sense to detect imminent terrorist action.

Since 2000, there have been nearly 70 terrorist incidents in the US, including the Sept, 11 attacks in 2001, the 2013 Boston Marathon bombing, the San Bernardino Christmas party shooting in 2015, in 2016, the mass killing at an Orlando nightclub, the shooting on Oct. 1, 2017-in Las Vegas Boulevard and on February 14th, 2018, the shooting at Marjory Stoneman Douglas High School in Parkland, Florida. In addition too many more.

Nightclubs can be targets for domestic terrorism. Always be alert and locate exits, Crowded, tourist filled places are magnets for terrorist attacks.

Avoiding becoming a terrorist victim

If a parcel is delivered at home that you were not waiting for, decline it.

Before you drive make sure your car is in good condition, just a simple look that nothing has been changed, touched or altered. Especially out of the country.

If the road traffic slow down and you can't tell why, locks your doors, close all the windows and at the first street coming up, make a turn and leave, just in case.

Particular situations are high-level of vulnerability for terrorist, locations wherever large crowds of people congregate, government buildings, military institutions, bus or train, major public events, arenas, games.

You must be more vigilant and suspicious outside the United States.

If an assault happens

Lie flat on the floor or behind any hard object that may protect you from gunfire. Don't budge until the firing stops. Be prepared, if the threat is coming closer, you may have to move, move in your stomach. When you believe is clear, leave, and don't stop for any motive. Let the police do the work.

If the shooter gets to you and there is no way out, and for sure is going to shoot you, then you need to fight, move, throw anything at him, yell at someone imaginary looking at a door or window, trick him, for a few seconds to strike him or move for a better cover. Do anything it takes to get out of his firing spread; if worth comes to worth, maybe your last resort is to play dead.

If a terrorist attack occurs and you are trapped under debris

1-Cover your mouth.
2-Tap on a pipe or wall so that rescuers can hear you.
3-Shout only when you hear sounds so you don't run out of air

Chemical Attack

If you are indoors, you should

1-Close/ lock windows and exterior doors.

2-Keep your pets inside with you, keep pets under your direct control in case you have to evacuate.

3-Turn off all ventilation, air conditioners, vents, and fans.

4-Try to seal with duct tape, around doors, windows, vents, around pipes and off drains or other such openings.

5-Listen to radio or television recommendations until you are told all is safe or you are told to evacuate.

If you are outdoors

1-Move to shelter indoors immediately.

2-Listen to your local radio or television station for instructions from local officials.

Self-defense is not only our right; it is our duty
Ronald Reagan

Hostage's situations

If carrying weapons group seizes the location you are in, get out no matter what, do it fast, run away and don't run in a straight line, try to run in a Zigzag way, lessening the odds of getting shot. Run even if you get shout. The objective of nearly all terrorists is to apprehend a large group and use them for ransom, and at the end kill as many as possible.

If taken hostage and you don't have any other options, some experts think that personalizing yourself, like talking, about your children, mother or loved ones, presenting yourself as a caring, good person will help you, the strategy is that is harder to kill someone that you know that a stranger. Personally and don't believe this. This is something you have to make the decision yourself if you ever get into this situation. I hope not.

Stay calm, evaluate the circumstances, and prepare a plan in your mind, to put it into action, so you can attempt to save your life and the lives of your love ones.
If you grab a Taxi overseas, take the time to verify and check the driver picture with the photo on the license put on display in the car.

Coordinate non-stop flights.

Dress with not attention-grabbing clothes.

Do not mark with specific information your travelers' luggage.

As soon as checking in for your flight, proceed to the safeguarded section of the airport.

Without delay as soon as you arrive at your destination, get your baggage and leave the airport as quickly as possible.

Always be alert when you are at an airport, keeps your eyes open for abandon bags, luggage and packages.
If you realize something it is wrong, tell a police officer and leave right away.

He will win who knows when to fight and when not to fight
Sun Tzu

Personal Security

If possible travel, with others.

Prevent places that are customary visit with western travelers, places obvious aim for terrorism.

Every place you visit, keep a plan in mind in case of a bomb or terrorist attack.

Memorize phone numbers in case you lose your cell phone or it gets broken. Especially the phone number of the USA embassy.

Don't trust any stranger, Taxi drivers, hotel workers, anybody.

Select your own taxi; never get into a vehicle that is not marked as a Taxi.

When talking be alert who is listening and paying attention to your conversation, be aware.

Arrange meeting with strangers in public areas, if possible never in your hotel or room.

"Imagination is more important than knowledge"
Albert Einstein

Terrorism at workplace

You don't have to live in paranoia, but in today's world with so numerous occurrences it is a good idea to be aware.

1-Learn all the emergency exit doors at work, check were all takes you to, outside, floor, lobby, which one takes out of the building or the parking lot.

2-Check closets.

3-Learn where the phone is located.

4-Which office or area is more safety to get to if an intruder or employee is acting irrational?

5-Windows, check them all, where they exist to, if you use any of them to getaway, where can you exit from there or leap to?

6-Research the elevator; does it take you out to the parking lot? To the roof or penthouse? As soon as you step to the roof is there any place to hide or move to?

7-Look for a location that is not easy to find.

8-Verify the remote point from the main lobby, elevator, and exit door.

9-Test the closet door, emergency exit door to the lobby parking lot, garage.

10-Learn where the emergency buttons to fire alarm are located.

Terror attacks count on the scare of the victims. They create their thoughts on the notion that as soon as they rush into the location yelling, people will run or freeze, letting them do what they want. They never anticipate to be attacked. When you counterattack, you force them into a strategy changing plot, they have probably not planned for. Using this moment for you to fight, escape, or hide.

In a terrorist attack, you have only three ways to cope with the situation: to run if you can, hide as far as you can, or fight if your life is in imminent danger.

If you hide, silence your cell phone. Remain quiet, be alert, ready to escape, run or fight.

If your life is in danger and you don't have another alternative, fight hard and strong, use anything you can use, a broom stick, a stapler, glass of coffee, a chair anything you can use as an improvise weapon.

Call 911 when you are safe.

"Courage is being scared to death... and saddling up anyway"
John Wayne

Lone Wolf

The US law enforcement agencies and the media refer to "lone wolf" to comment on individuals who prepare and executes violent acts alone, with no material support from any group and without a command group. He or she may be motivated by the philosophy of a group, and may commit violent acts in support of such a group.

This is the mindset of a loner who see himself as a hero, often do not give any signs to people around them of what they are planning or capable of doing. Attacks quickly, most of the time strike places or individual they know. Very hard to, predict and very dangerous.

Wolves are solitary individuals; they normally avoid contact with others. This makes extremely difficult for authorities to identify and arrest them. Since they work alone, there are no means of communication to intercept or accomplices to detain and question. This type of terrorist attack has been increasing in number recently.

Expert claims there are five basic types, secular, religious, single-issue, criminal, and idiosyncratic, probably many lone wolves fall into two or three categories.

Secular lone wolves, carry out violent attacks for political, ethnic-nationalist, like secular terrorist groups do.
The religious lone wolf commits terrorism in the name of religious belief system.
The single-issue lone wolf perpetrates attacks in the name of any particular issue, such as abortion, animal rights, or the environment.

The criminal lone wolf is encouraged by money. Experts believe because of a lack of ideological motive they do not consider lone-wolf criminals to be terrorists.

The idiosyncratic lone wolf is motivated by personal demons. However, he may perpetrate an attack in the name of a specific motive, those reasons are often irrational.

Workplace violence, assaults

Warning signs:

Stressed changes in attitude, behavior and work ethic.

Suddenly quiet and reserved, it could be a sign

FBI's National Center Analysis of Violent Crime passed incidents, at the workplace.

Hostile, troubling, bullying and aggressive behavior

Tensions with supervisors and other employees

New interest with weapons

Declarations revealing praise of the use of violence to solve problems

Statements desperation over family, financial, other personal problems,

Contemplating suicide

Drug/alcohol abuse

Extreme changes in behavior

Flash-mob Riot

An angry mob is frightening and erratic, I was in one in Bolivia, and Mexico City many years ago, and it is not fun. You might get hurt fast and easy. What makes a mob dangerous is that they don't have any fear of repercussions. This is not new, riots have been happening for many years.

This threat of violence happens in a split of a -second. The motivations can be ethnic, economic and political, by the time you sense an attack is occurring, you may only have minutes, or even seconds to get yourself or family to safety. Mobs are very dangerous, the group can create a powerful horde, caught in one can easily lead to injury or death.

Most of the time is a group of cowardly thugs to create a wave to steal and destroy without being caught. If you have a licensed weapon, do not show it. Someone may try to take it away from you, or attack you thinking you are there to stop them.

Keep in mind you can't resist a mob, instead try to escape it, fast locate the nearest escape street and get out fast.

You have to stay away from store fronts, the mob or anarchist is going to try to loot the stores around; Stores are magnets for violence and riots. Stay away from stores in a Mob-Riot!

If you're trapped in a riot, run alongside their path to avoid being crushed, try to reach and walk by one of the outside areas. Then, try to get out as quickly as you can, like a hotel lobby. Always avoid confrontation, if you walk, hold hands with the people you are with, so you won't get separated.

Don't look like an outsider target, yell if they are yelling, scream, like them, run if they are running, and without anybody realizing it move to safety slowly with caution. Make them believe you are a part of the riot. You must be very careful not to get confused for one of them by the police. You can explain later to the police, your escape plan. As you can see; this is very dangerous and particular risky situation.

Get out alive:

A-Lookout for indications that a demonstration may become a riot.

B-Get out from the region fast, at the first sign of trouble.

C-Don't ever drive your vehicle through a mob. No matter what, don't get involved.

D-Move away from police lines. You don't want to be trapped in the center of violence and the path where objects like bottles, rocks will be thrown. Never attempt to cross police lines to escape, the police are there to stop the disturbance spreading, and not to allow anyone to pass. Police may use riot tear gas, to dissolve a crowd. These gases will cause respiratory distress, and blindness. Try to stay away from the front lines of a riot.

E-Don't take shelter in a neighboring shop. It could become the aim of the violence. Go out through the rear exit if there is one.

F-Guard your head from things being thrown. A garbage can lid or other object alike on the street could work as a shield.

G-Protect yourself; don't stop to participate in anyone fight. Keep moving, and moving to safety.

H-Try to stay on your feet no matter what, to keep you from being trampled or battered.

I-Understand your State and local laws and how you can protect your own property.

J-If you are at home lock doors and windows and stay away from them, to avoid getting hurt by stones, bullets. Never confront the rioters or try to prevent property damage.

K-If you drop something, unless it's your cell phone, your work case, your wallet, or your compact computer, let it go, do not to pick it up; you could be crushed by the multitude.

> *The Second Amendment isn't about duck hunting or target shooting.*
>
> *Massad Ayoob*

Caught in a roadway mob Demonstration?

A roadway block does not cause death or injury to those inside the vehicle, but if it gets out of hand, can become a dangerous threat of death or injury to people in a vehicle. Stay in the car, and driving slowly if the mob is not assaulting your car. Don't stop for any reason unless you have to. Stick to less-traveled side streets to avoid the mobs. Try to avoid public transportation.

Become familiar with the vicinity where you work, live, and the option's streets between home and work. Get to know small less congested streets, in an emergency they are good to take.

Most individuals say they will use their car to run the mob down, or to force them aside; you will be in trouble with the law if someone gets hurt by you doing so. If the protesters are trying to go into the vehicle, or attacking you with a metal bar or with a baseball bat, now the scenario has changed. You are in fear of your life or the life of a family member. You would be permitted by law to use deadly force in self-defense, including the use of your vehicle to neutralize the deadly force threat.

You do not need to wait until the protesters have turned violent against your vehicle, if you see it happening to another car that is enough. This is the moment you may use your car for deadly force legally.

If your car becomes a target, leave it. Your car, truck are not worth dying for. The road is not for protester, no matter the motivation, is for vehicles. These crowds are breaking the law; most of these protesters don't have a permit allowing them to protest.

Tips

What to do if you encounter a mob?

Shift direction, and get out of the area as quickly as you can, drive
with caution and slowly, the wrong way even if you have to. If you
always stay alert, you will see these masses in advance so that you
can evade the situation, long before being surrounded.

If the mob assaults your car, roll down your windows half an inch,
experts say it is harder to smash a window that is partially down than
one that is fully closed. Set off your ventilation system so no outside,
tear gas or smoke air comes in. Unlock your seatbelt in case you need
to exit the car should it be rolled over or set on fire.

The proper action is to stay away from these demonstrations and drive
away at once should you come upon one. Evading is the key!

The strictest law sometimes becomes the severest injustice
Benjamin Franklin

Hijacking

In the 1990s, the United States Department of State's Overseas Security Advisory Council established a set of individual security guidelines for American business travelers overseas, containing how to respond to a hijacking scenario.

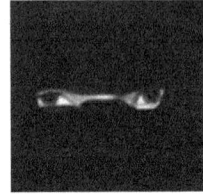

Here are some tips:
A- Stay calm.
B- Keep in mind that the hijackers are nervous and most likely scared.
C- Obey your captors' commands.
D- If shooting takes place, keep head low and body down to the floor.
E- Stay aware.

What to do Throughout the Negotiation Phase of a Hijacking:
1-If you are told to keep your head down, do it.
2-Prepare mentally for a long ordeal.
3-Do not try to hide your passport or belongings.
4-If spoke by the hijackers, respond in a calm tone of voice.

If a rescue operation occurs, will involve noise, chaos, shooting, and you must follow the following.
What to do During a Hostage Rescue Operation:

A-If you hear shots fired inside or outside the aircraft, immediately put your head down or drop to the floor.
B-If ordered by the rescue to run, do it, place your hands up in the air or behind your head.
C-Make no unexpected move.
D-If any smoke appears, get to an emergency exits door, open it, and exit onto the wing.
E-When reaching the tarmac, follow the instructions of local authorities; move as quickly as possible away from the aircraft, moving towards the terminal or a control tower area.
Probably initially you will be treated roughly until it is determined by the rescue militant that you are not part of the hijacking team.

The New Assault Trend

Cyber Concern

Remember when you received an e-mail from overseas dignitary in Nigeria? Or an American trapped overseas somewhere? By now all of us have gotten many times similar text or e-mail.
Believe or not, many people believed it the past when the scam just came out.

Spy-ware is used to collect data from a computer with no knowledge of the user. It makes you believe that is an authentic download, allowing the hackers remotely to entry your computer to acquire private info. Scams use all kinds of false websites, and offers.

Your home can be protected, but there is an open gate –The World Wide Web. Millions of debit card are robbed every year, phone numbers, full names and addresses.

Millions of Identities have been stolen, remember Home Depot had 56 million credit card numbers stolen in 2014; others like TJX, Marshall also had credit cards stolen.

The Internet can be disturbing and cost you money if you are not careful.

Tips:

Under no circumstances disclose your password, account information with anybody over the net.
Be suspicious of callers, pop-ups, or e-mails questioning for private information.
Change your safe passwords frequently.
Under no circumstances download software from an individual or companies you don't know.
Check your account statements and credit card reports often.

Cyberbullying

Today Bullying has moved from the park or school playground into Cyberspace. Not only between kids, but also bullying between adults.

Professionals believe Cyberbullying can be more damaging, psychologically that physically. "Targets often do not know who the bully is, or why they are being targeted", says Sameer Hinduja, Ph.D., co-director of the Cyberbullying Research Center. "The aggressor can cloak his or her identity behind a computer or cell phone using an anonymous email address or pseudonymous names"

Today there is a lot of argument in Facebook or in the comments section, including political, religious, many times between friends, people becomes victims of online harassment.

1-About one in four women's ages 18 to 24 have been stalked or sexually harassed on the Internet.

2-According to experts 21% of students between ages 12 to 18 in the US have been bullied online.

3-About 40% of adults have been bullied or harassed online.

Steps to stop and handle online Bullying

Do not reply to Cyberbully.
This is going to worsen the situation. If you decide to answer, you can ask the person to stop bullying.

Keep all the proof.
Take screen pictures, keep voice mail and print, photocopies of emails and text.

Report the harassment.
Check the privacy social media control center sites to be familiar with about their regulations, and complaint.

Contact law enforcement.
Notified them of the threats, physical harm and or sexual harassment, stalking.

Block the Bully.
Block the bully's social media profiles, emails and phone numbers.

Safeguard your passwords.
Change them right away and don't tell anyone the new one.

Check your privacy controls.
Be absolutely sure that only people you are familiar with and trust can see your social media.

Nobody can hurt me without my permission
Mahatma Gandhi

Safety Tips in Cyberspace

The Internet is very educational and entertaining, everybody agrees, but it is also very dangerous if you are not careful. Use should always use a nickname, **don't give out personal information** such as home address, phone number, and keep them confidential.

If you too like to meet new people over the net like boyfriends and girlfriends, be careful. When you do meet them do it in a **public place** and always take someone with you for the first couples of times.

Don't trust them, don't believe anything until it's been a while and you got to know them better. Don't invite them over your house, don't tell them where you work or live for a while.

When you go out with one of these people make sure to **tell someone** where you are going, and planning to come back.

Ask a friend to **call** you a couple of times during this night out, in case you need to make an excuse and need to leave.

This way the friend can keep an eye on you. Believe me; it could save your life if you get caught with the wrong person.

Do not believe anything you heard, don't go anyplace with him/them, till you get to know these people and even so, always tell a friend where, the time, and possibly make of car, color, and time of arrival.

Chapter 8-Final thoughts

You must keep in mind that there is a big possibility that when you get complicated in a self-defense situation you are going to get injured. Is a must to keep in mind how strong or weak you are, if you are weak or small no doubt about it, you are at a big disadvantage. The more you know about yourself, your strength, agility, speed, the better.

Keep in mind that a street fight is unpredictable and is continually changing. You cannot get ready for one because it can happen at the most unexpected moment and in a way you never believe could happen and in most of the cases it's over with one or two moves. Sometime even before you know it is over.

In a street fight most likely your opponent could be under the influence of drugs, or drunk, possibly he is carrying a weapon. Likely he is going to be much stronger than you. You must be prepared yourself for this situation and ask yourself how you are going to handle it if it ever comes up.

If you are arguing with an attacker, you must pay close attention to dangerous signs like, is he clenching his fist? Does he have other friends close by? Does he have a weapon? Does he is holding a beer bottle in his hand or a pen? A bottle or a pen could be a weapon. A keychain is a weapon. Do you understand now what I mean? Maybe he is at odds with you and he has his keys in his hand to use it as a weapon against you and you did not realize it. Is he in shape?

How big he is compared to you? If you decided to run, where would you run? Can you be faster than him? Would you be able to escape? Keep in mind that criminals are looking for easy targets and most of the time they will try to intimidate you with their looks, clothes, body type, tattoos, etc. He will use vulgar language; name calling, insults and gestures to complete intimidated you.

Do not let him do it. No matter how frightful or intimidated he seems he have vulnerable body parts just like you do.

Conclusion of violent consequences

Call 911 and if you are hurt request an ambulance. Explain to arriving officers all the details you remember.

Victims of violence develop post-traumatic symptoms; emotional distress may make you experience sleeping problems, isolation and depression. Also, will be taxing on your family, marriages, and many times marriage will be destroyed.

 Make no declaration to the press. It is a good idea to contact a good lawyer in case you needed to have representation.

Knowledge will give you power, but character respect
Bruce Lee

These tips will help protect you, your loved ones - and may even save your life!

1. Make sure that all doors and windows are locked, including the garage door when you leave home every day.

2. Do not carry large sums of money. Possible carry small bills.

3. If possible, don't travel alone. Particularly at night.

4. Carry anything valuable in your pocket not in your purse or wallet. Always leave all unnecessary credit cards at home.

5. Drive at night through only well-lighted and well-traveled streets. Don't take shortcuts.

6. Never ever give rides or accept rides from strangers.

7. If you have to walk, walk on the side of the street closer to oncoming traffic. If someone in a car molested you, run in the direction opposite the way the car is headed.

8. Stay very careful with people asking directions; keep a safe distance. This is very, very important.

9. When you return home, do not waste time at the entrance of your home. Check your mail, if it's too late, leave the mail for tomorrow. If you sense something is not normal, don't enter, move quickly out of there, go elsewhere and call for police assistance.

10. If you feel someone is following you walking, walk to the nearest residence or building, and ask for help or to call the police.

11. If you are confronted with a dangerous situation, do not hesitate to cry out for help the faster the better, not given the attacker anytime to grab you or shock you. Yelling "FIRE! FIRE!" instead of "Help!"

> *Quickness is the essence of the war*
> *Sun Tzu*

Putting it all together

It was very hard for me to finish this book. It seems like there it was always one more thing to tell you. The truth is you can never say it all. What I have mentioned in this book is in general and maybe do not apply to all of you.

Learn what you can use, discard the rest like the famous Jeet-Kune Do master Bruce Lee use to say. The choice must come from you, the reader. You must make a decision of what action to take and how far to take it. Nobody can do it for you.

The Author- Frank Marchante younger years

Select three techniques and combinations of the one you think you will be able to use, practice it every time you can until you can perform them without thinking.
 In an emergency keep repeating them over and over, fast. That's all you need.

You should do the combination of your choice with your eyes closed, practicing it many times to develop the feel for defense.
Don't allow yourself to be a victim. Your attacker abides by no rules and neither should you.

My greatest hope is this book does more than build specific awareness tactics that I describe here, but you can create safety habits of your own for the rest of your life.

"Absorb what is useful, Discard what is not, Add what is uniquely your own."

Bruce Lee

Note:

This book was written with down-to-earth principle to make easy its techniques. You are the reader must make acquainted yourself with the concepts of awareness assertiveness and apply its principles in daily personal life!

With this proven and easy-to-use training formula described in my book, you will find out amazing secrets on how to escape to safety, or to strike, when and how with minimal physical training and effort!

This Book could save your Life!

The real world of street fighting has no rules!
Good Luck!

About the Author

Frank Marchante has been a student and an enthusiastic of the martial arts since 1964, and has practiced for over 50 years.

He began learning karate when he was 13 years old, later changes style to Wing Chun kun-Fu training, for many years, at the same time his father taught him how to box.

Had his share of real street fights, as youth belonging to a Fraternity (gang) of 45 members, during the middle of the 1960s.

The Author has traveled, visited, and walked by many cities and dangerous neighborhoods, where he refined his safety approach.

As an educator and a generalist Marchante has read significantly about many topics, and have met extraordinary people, and tried new endeavors. He wanted to experience the world broadly. And he has.

Frank has participated in many adventures, accomplishing ascents to one of the tallest peaks, most impressive mountain in Bolivia, 21,000 feet high, Illimani, one of the highest mountain peaks in the Andes, the eighteenth highest peak in South America, using an oxygen mask to reach one of the top summits, walking through the clouds sometimes in the snow all the way pass his knees.

The Author ventured deep by foot into the deep, dark, and dense, dangerous and inevitably Amazon Jungle in Bolivia's /Peru. Drove through the World's Most Dangerous Road Bolivia –The Death Road in 1971. Marchante traveled across the intimidating Titicaca Lake, the highest lake in the world in an Indian canoe, accompanied by an Indian from Bolivia to Peru, 46 years ago, before tourists begins visiting the lake.

He climbed the massive volcano of Popocatepetl, Mexico, the second highest in Mexico and North America's 2nd highest volcano at 5,452 meters (17,887 feet) above sea level. He has also Hang –glide from a very high peak Mountain in Acapulco city and also has done parasailing in Acapulco and Cozumel.

The Author took his first flying lessons in the early 70s in Tamiami airport in South Miami in a Piper Cherokee 140, where at the end of the 80s kept his own plane, a Panther 2.

In 1986, he applied to NASA when the Teacher's educator space program to go into space in the shuttle Challenger, he was not chosen. The shuttle exploded 73 seconds after liftoff.

Marchante has always enjoyed racing motorcycles, has owned many through his life and still owns one, a Honda 1970 Bonneville 750cc antique with cruise control.

He is very adventurous, like speed and action; he owned a 15-foot speed racing boat that can carry three people aboard.

Frank was one of 30 teachers selected in North America to participate in the People to People Ambassador Program in his delegation and Technical Education advisor to the Republic of China in February 2001.

Frank Marchante was a Florida educator, Pear teacher and head of Department for 30 years, he is retired now.

He has writing for newspapers and magazines, written several songs, he is the author of published books like Sergio Oliva the Myth, Marchante Home Inspection, El Atentado del Siglo (The Ultimate Target) there are many pages on the internet from Russia to France discussing his books and you can catch an interview with him at Bodybuilding.com.

In 2004, he was the speaker and the recipient of "The Hall of Fame" Award for Sergio Oliva on Feb. 2004, and the speaker who introduced Sergio Oliva at the south Florida Bodybuilding Championship.

Memory Lane-Author Life Pictures

The author has taught thousands of teenagers

Horsing around with a student

Memory Lane-Author Life Pictures

Receiving an award

Tamiami Airport-Miami, FL-Proud owner of a Panther2+

Younger Years-Motorcycle Association

Illimani Bolivia mountain peak

Appalachian Trail MTN.GA with son, Franky

277

Knowledge Wordlists

Aggravated assault- producing bodily injury.

Aggressor- the person perpetrating an aggression.

Ambush zones- places to hide and wait to launch a surprise assault.

Assault and battery- to make a sudden, violent attack on someone.

Attack- the act of attacking with physical force.

Alley-a narrow back street, between or behind buildings.

Automatic Pistol- empty the shell, puts a new one, to be fired again.

Awareness- the state or condition of being aware, consciousness.

Burglary- the entering of a building with the intent to commit a crime.

Conflict- discord of one idea, opposition, of principles.

Crook- dishonest person, especially, someone who cheats or steals.

Deadly force-the last resort, when all lesser means have failed.

Deadly weapon-guns, knives, when used to cause injury.

Delinquent-a person who regularly performs illegal or immoral acts.

Excessive force-force beyond the need for a specific conflict.

Escape-get away, avoid capture.

Equalizer-people, the thing that equalizes, balance opposing forces.

Flash-mob- group who assembles public, act bizarre, and disperses.

Fear-emotion aroused by impending danger, anticipate something.

Fight-battle or single combat; defend, defeat, destroy an adversary.

Killer instinct-natural instinct inside each of us, a source of energy.

Knife -essentially a thin, sharp-edged, metal blade with a handle.

Lethal force- force to cause bodily injury or death to another person.

Long wolf- criminals who act alone, person who lives, acts, work alone.

Rape- forces a person to submit to sexual intercourse.

Revolver- revolving chambered cylinder for holding cartridges.

Reaction- action in response to some influence, event, etc.

Scare- suddenly, with fear or terror, frightens alarm.

Self-defense- defending one person when physically attacked.

Strike- blow, stroke to a person with the fist, or a weapon,

Shotgun -smoothbore gun for hunting.

Sucker-Punch -unexpected surprise punch, mainly from behind.

Punch- a thrusting blow, especially with the fist.

Terrorist- a member of a group, who uses or advocates terrorism.

Terrorism- violence to intimidate or coerce, for political purposes.

Victim- a person who has suffered the effects of violence.

Violence- extremely forceful actions intended to hurt people.

Photo Credit:

Protector

It's tough starting high school. Everybody deals with classes, friends, and crushes but fifteen year old Sakura has more on her plate: She has to deal with a hereditary transformation which only takes place when the Earth is in great danger.

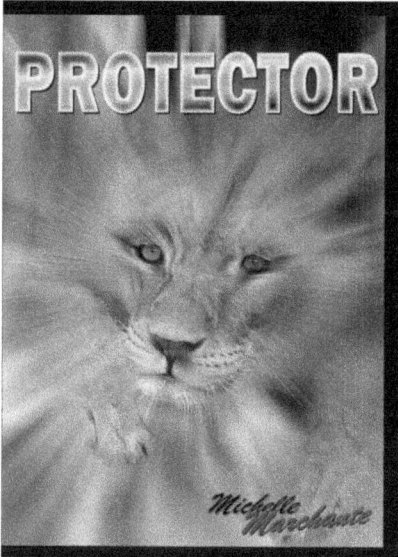

Looking to her ancestors for guidance and training, keeping it secret from loved ones, as she prepares to go fight the threat: Master and his Minions in hopes of saving her planet.

Including her heart's dilemma: Austin or Roy? Who will she choose? The clock is ticking... Will she be able to find the strength and courage to save the world from total destruction? Will she ever make up her mind between Austin and Roy!

An intriguing tale of adventure, danger, romance, and a little thing called high school! For every book sold a donation will be made to a wildlife foundation.

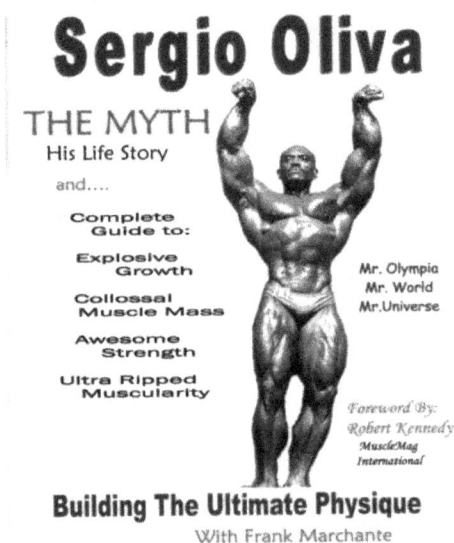

Gras Publishing Present
Visit www.graspublishing.com

EL ATENTADO DEL SIGLO

BY FRANK MARCHANTE

Un trama trepidante y llena de suspenso..... Caracterización intrigante.
Basado en una historia real, alterado con algo de ficticia, toma a los lectores de sorpresa, llena el corazón de suspenso y angustioso pulso, fuerte, ya sea en tierra o en el mar. Este suspenso de gran éxito, se establece a 90 millas de USA.
Un hombre de la CIA infiltrado en Cuba con una misión para ajusticiar a Fidel Castro, un hombre con un dedo en el gatillo de su arma puede cambiar la historia.....

Repleto de acción, suspenso y los personajes reales, humanos con una caracterización increíble.

El autor de este apasionante relato, cuya identidad, por razones obvias, debe permanecer en secreto contó su historia a Frank Marchante que lo trajo a la vida, trasfirió, le añadió alguna ficticia y organizo en papel. Los nombres a través del libro son igualmente ficticios por la misma razón.

No importa si todos los datos son ciertos o no. Emocionante e imaginativa, llena de acción y la intriga aumenta el pulso, teniendo a lectores en una aventura salvaje.

No es ningún secreto que la CIA estuvo involucrada en una variedad de proyectos, para llevar a cabo la eliminación de Fidel Castro. Este es un relato fascinante en primera persona de un proyecto de la CIA para eliminar a Fidel Castro, de la realización de una acción encubierta en secreto que detalla las mentiras y engaños de la agencia.

Una de la mayor acción jamás encubierta y en secreto realizada. Se lee casi como una novela de suspenso y aventura.
Incluye crónica de la Revolución de los últimos 55 años, también presenta parte de la historia de cuba.

Notes